Centennial Farm Family

Cultivating Land and Community: 1837 - 1937

Amy McVay Abbott

Centennial Farm Family

Cultivating Land and Community: 1837 - 1937

Amy McVay Abbott

ISBN: 9780578885285
First Edition June 28, 2021

In Memoria

For LeNore Alice Hoard Enz, "Grammy"
June 28, 1908 – April 22, 1994
Great-granddaughter of Reuben and Elizabeth Long.

About the Book Title

In 1947, LeNore Alice Hoard Enz received a Centennial Farm Family
designation from the Indiana Historical Society. Her first cousin Berniece Long
Piepho also received recognition. Both women were great-granddaughters of Reuben
and Elizabeth Olinger Long, who came to Whitley County from Montgomery
County, Ohio, in the 1830s. Both LeNore and Berniece were awarded a bronze
seal, signifying a century-old family farm's continuous ownership. Each inherited
half the acreage of the legacy farm.

Table of Contents

The Family

Kellis Hord
B: BET 1795 AND 1810 USA
M: 15 May 1839 Ohio, USA
D: Cleveland, Ohio, USA

John Tyler Hoard
B: 03/04/1840 Ohio, USA
M: 26 Oct 1865 United States
D: 01 NOV 1902 Indiana, USA

Angelina More
B: ABT 1820 Virginia, USA
M: 15 May 1839 Ohio, USA
D: Bakersville, Ohio, USA

Henry Kellis Hoard
B: 1 Mar 1870 Indiana
M: 1899 Indiana, United States
D: 2 Dec 1932 Fort Wayne, Indiana, USA

Christian Henry Creager
B: 16 Aug 1821 . Ohio, USA
M: 30 DEC 1841 Indiana, USA
D: 20 May 1906 Indiana, USA

Peter Creager
B: 21 AUG 1777 Maryland, USA
D: 16 MAR 1849 Indiana, USA

Elizabeth Rike (Reichman)
B: 21 (26?) Jan 1790 USA
D: 5 Apr 1870 Indiana, USA

Catherine (Kate) Creager
B: 16 JAN 1845 Indiana, USA
M: 26 Oct 1865 United States
D: 15 JUL 1835 Indiana, USA

Susanah Obenchain
B: 26 October 1822 USA
M: 30 DEC 1841 Indiana, USA
D: 12 Nov 1862 , Indiana, USA

Samuel Obenchain
B: 1 May 1797 Virginia, USA
D: 24 May 1869 Indiana, USA

Catharine Flora
B: 19 July 1802 Virginia, USA
D: 23 Mar 1849 United States

LeNore Alice Hoard
B: 28 June 1908 Whitley County, Indiana, USA
M: 12 Apr 1931 st. paul lutheran church, Fort Wayne, …
D: 22 April 1994 Fort Wayne, Allen, Indiana, USA

Reuben Long
B: 5 April 1801 Virginia
M: 4 Aug 1824 Ohio, USA
D: 19 June 1861 Indiana

Lewis Long
B: 1770 Virginia
D: 25 Mar 1848

Catherine Hiestand
B: 1777
D: 25 Aug 1870 Indiana

Washington Long
B: abt 1846 Indiana
M: 9 Sep 1871 United States
D: 1 September 1930 Indiana, USA

Elizabeth Olinger
B: 11 SEP 1803 United States
M: 4 Aug 1824 Ohio, USA
D: 28 Feb 1870 Indiana

Jacob Olinger
B: 4 May 1777 Pennsylvania, USA
D: 1855 Indiana, USA

Maria Susannah
B: 1777 Pennsylvania, USA
D: 1840 OH, USA

Anna Long
B: abt 1877 Indiana
M: 1899 Indiana, United States
D: 30 Jun 1937 Tunker, Indiana, USA

Jonas Baker
B: 17 Feb 1822 Ohio, USA
M: 28 May 1843 Ohio, USA
D: 15 Jul 1890 Indiana, USA

Daniel Baker
B: 1 Aug 1785 United States
D: 10 Jul 1872 United States

Elizabeth Bucks '
B: 9 Aug 1781 Pennsylvania, USA
D: Clay, Montgomery, Ohio, USA

Mary Jane Baker
B: 15 July 1852 Indiana
M: 9 Sep 1871 United States
D: 1880 Whitley County, Indiana

Mariah Haines
B: 24 Nov 1821 USA
M: 28 May 1843 Ohio, USA
D: 4 Oct 1887 Indiana, USA

Curtis Haines '
B: 1793 Pennsylvania, USA
D: 10 March 1868

Margaret
B: abt 1794 PA., USA
D: 5 April 1871 OH., USA

Preface

This book traces the lineage of four generations of my maternal grandmother's family. My grandmother, LeNore Hoard Enz, fostered my interest in history, especially family history. She was proud of her ancestors and loved sharing their tales and adventures. She also encouraged others to tell their stories of pioneer days.

The book's title comes from an award given to the legacy farm in 1947. My grandmother and her first cousin, Berniece Long Piepho, received Centennial Farm Family awards from the Indiana Historical Society. Each cousin inherited half of the legacy farm from their grandfather Washington Long. Each received a bronze plaque for the farm's century-long continuous ownership. My grandparents hung the bronze plaque proudly on their farmhouse door.

My grandmother, who died in 1994, left volumes of information. Some items had "for Amy LeNore" scribbled on them, in Grammy's handwriting, as soon as 1958 when I was a toddler. She started encouraging me early!

Family members elected me the keeper of the flame. I am humbled to carry these stories forward for future generations. These stories come from oral histories, letters, documents, newspaper articles, deeds, wills, affidavits, pictures, programs, yearbooks, maps, city directories, and history books. I read dozens of books and hundreds of newspaper articles to learn about when plum trees bloomed or when Whitley County farms acquired telephones. City maps and directories clued me in on where businesses were located. Event programs, yearbooks, legal documents, and history books gave me details that were outside family stories. I've done my best to present an accurate portrayal of a century that ended twenty years before my birth.

1

Every writer of historical nonfiction struggles with period-specific language now considered offensive. I chose historical accuracy and included words now considered derogatory. I do not condone or encourage the use of these words today; the choice reflects historical usage.

In sharing my ancestors' trials and triumphs, my goal is that readers find commonality with their family stories. It was important to me to tell the entire stories in the times in which they happened. For our children and our communities, there is value in preserving what otherwise may be lost.

—Amy LeNore McVay Abbott, June 2021

Introduction, 1932

KELLIS AND ANNA HOARD, 1932.

Anna Long Hoard stood beside her dying husband at Lutheran Hospital, numb with grief and disbelief. Two days earlier, Kellis Hoard had been a robust and healthy man of 62. Now, he lay dying because of a careless mistake.

Unsteady, Anna grasped the metal bed frame, in fear exhaustion would cause her to pass out. Thoughts of life without Kellis swept over her in waves. In their 37 years of marriage, they rarely spent a night apart. Anna was uncertain how she could live without her husband.

Kellis, whose full name was Henry Kellis Hoard, worked on land that had been in Anna's family since her grandparents Reuben and Elizabeth Long moved from Ohio in the 1830s. Most farmers' wealth and livelihood were secured in their legacy land, intended to sustain them, their children, and their children's children. But the Hoards had no sons, and their daughters had moved away.

The Hoards, their neighbors, and most Hoosiers had struggled with finances since the end of World War I. Farmers had produced government-requested excess crops for the war effort. When the war ended, farm prices crashed. The reward for a farmer's patriotism was excess grain he couldn't sell and storage fees at the local elevator. Out of necessity, Kellis and Anna obtained a mortgage loan of $4,000 in 1922. Farm prices stayed low throughout the 1920s.

Kellis took a second job for extra income at Perry Yoder's store, a stone's throw from the farm. Yoder found him a considerable asset— Kellis knew everyone, and everyone knew him. Kellis supported 4-H Clubs, the Whitley County Fair, and was an officer for the Farmers' Elevator and the local Farm Bureau. He was always the first in line to help a neighbor or his community.

Now the community's good neighbor was in trouble.

In winter, farmers gathered at Yoder's Store on weekday afternoons. In heavy-weight bib overalls, men hashed over politics, grain prices, and spring planting. The store was a jumble of products, soaps, medicines, notions, ammunition, fishing tackle, fertilizer components, and penny nails. Stacked cases of everything from tomato soup to hammers dotted the wooden floors. Yoder kept spittoons for his customers near the black pot-bellied stove in the front room. Between spitting part of their chaw and telling tall tales, the men snuck into the storeroom for a taste of home-brew. What Prohibition outlawed in 1919—bootleg whiskey, hooch, hard cider, moonshine—was available all over Whitley County. Men slipped into the dimly-lighted storeroom for a nip of hard cider from the solitary jug always on the counter.

Kellis, an occasional tippler, grabbed the jug in the storeroom. Every man in the store had snuck into the backroom for a nip at one time or another. Kellis hoisted the familiar stoneware container and took a swig from its tiny, rounded mouth.

What he tasted was nothing like what he expected. The drink burned his mouth and throat, fiery hot, like lightning blazing through ripe standing wheat.

He shoved the jug aside and stumbled back into the front room, triggering the attention of the men crowded around the pot-bellied stove. Something was very wrong.

All eyes in the crowded front room turned to Kellis, bent double. His neighbors lay Kellis on the floor.

A quarter of a mile down Tunker Road, Anna's kitchen warmed the entire downstairs as she prepared dinner for her husband and the hired man. Anna removed the bread from her wood stove, placing the fragrant loaves to cool on her Hoosier cabinet. Tonight's dinner would be hearty; Kellis would be chilly, even after his walk home.

The wooden party line telephone, hanging on the kitchen wall, rang— two longs, two shorts.

"Anna, come to the store; your husband has had an accident," an unknown voice shouted into the phone and hung up.

What accident could happen at the store, Anna thought. Like all farmers, Kellis faced many dangers—a limb catching in equipment, a bucking horse, or tripping into a hole. What farmer had not encountered a poisonous snake or two in the haymow or a cornfield? Farm life was inherently dangerous.

But the store? Kellis ran the cash register, unloaded boxes from delivery trucks, and counted inventory. None of what Anna had heard on the phone made sense. Anna pulled on a barn coat over her housedress and grabbed her galoshes. She would not leave the house dressed in work clothes under ordinary circumstances. These were hardly normal circumstances; Anna ran the quarter-mile down Tunker Road to the store.

A neighbor stood in icy puddles near the store, waiting for her. He shouted, "Kellis drank something that might have been poison."

Anna entered through the double wooden doors and saw a crush of men hovering over someone on the floor. Kellis was moaning and writhing in pain, lying on the plank floor between crates of tomato soup and canned pears.

Neighbors carried Kellis, trembling in agony, through the store into someone's truck. Another man ran back into the storeroom and grabbed the jug Kellis drank from, corking the top so the remaining liquid wouldn't drain out. Maybe the fluid could be identified at the hospital. Onlookers, talking in low voices and shaking their heads, flocked outside, watching the truck and its injured passenger head towards the county seat. The neighbor drove Anna and Kellis ten miles to the nearest hospital in Columbia City.

Anna held her husband's hand and wiped his brow. She asked the driver about the jug in the storeroom. The neighbor said no one had any idea what had happened. It was so odd no one at the store became ill.

Physicians at Columbia City sent Kellis by ambulance to the Lutheran Hospital. The larger, better equipped Fort Wayne hospital was only 20 miles away, but icy roads slowed the trip. Still in her housedress, Anna rode with her husband in the back of the ambulance.

At the hospital, she held a vigil at her husband's side for hours as he weaved in and out of consciousness. Doctors gave Anna little hope for Kellis's recovery. Even at the highest recommended dose, morphine barely relieved his suffering. He could not swallow pills; his throat and stomach burned. Nurses injected him with their most potent opioid every two hours, but the shots only skimmed the surface of the pain from his throat and below.

Anna dozed in fits and starts in a chair near her husband's hospital bed on Wednesday night. Did she dream of other losses as she worried about her husband? Did she think of their middle daughter, Mae, who died in a car accident a decade earlier? Did she dream of her brother, Franklin, lost in a farm accident when Anna was a teenager?

Anna awoke to find her oldest daughter, Zoe Hoard, leaning over Kellis's bed. Zoe, an elementary school principal, left near dawn for the

90-minute drive to Fort Wayne from South Bend. Anna was grateful to see her eldest child. Zoe was the organizer, the peacemaker, the comforter.

LeNore Enz, the younger daughter, arrived later Thursday from Springfield, Illinois, drained from travel. Unlike her older, more practical sister, LeNore could be frantic and disorganized. Anna was comforted by both daughters' presence, even though they sometimes fought as sisters do.

Carl Enz, LeNore's husband, had loaded their Buick with clothes and the couple's two daughters on Wednesday evening. The family drove more than 300 miles in wintry weather on poor roads. After leaving LeNore at the Fort Wayne hospital, Carl went to his parents' house on Alabama Street, ready for rest and help with his daughters, Donna Enz, four, and Marilyn Enz, an infant.

Kellis continued his life-and-death struggle Thursday night. Anna stood at her husband's bedside with her daughters when the doctor called Kellis's death at 5:35 a.m., Friday, not 48 hours after the accident. LeNore, a registered nurse, helped the attending nurse pull the sheet over Kellis's face. LeNore had trained as a nurse at Lutheran Hospital graduating in 1929. The small act of drawing the sheet over her father devastated LeNore. She adored her father. And she had been Kellis's favorite, an open secret in the family.

A hospital pharmacist identified the jug's contents as sulphuric acid, an ingredient in fertilizer, corrosive enough to put holes in the stomach, cause blindness, and severely burn the throat and esophagus. The death certificate listed as cause of death "edema of the glottis" and "stricture of the esophagus" and noted Kellis accidentally drank sulphuric acid mistaken for cider—a euphemism for alcohol. Why the unlikely poisoning happened remains a mystery.

❦

Anna and her daughters soon busied with funeral details, with South Whitley's Miller and Pook Funeral Home handling the arrangements. Kellis would be laid to rest at Eberhard Lutheran Church, near their daughter Mae. Thoughts of standing beneath a tent at the cemetery gave Anna a chill. How could she stand to watch her husband's casket drop into the ground so near the grave of their dear Mae?

Anna couldn't help but think of her father, gone such a short time. She wished Washington Long were still alive so she could hold his steady arm at the funeral and committal. On Sunday, she would witness the burial of her husband, one of the two most important men in her life. Anna had enjoyed a close relationship with her father. Anna and Washington always depended on each other for strength. Now both these men were gone from her life.

Despite her small stature, Anna possessed a sizeable toughness and fortitude unmatched by others. The new widow knew she could and would draw on the love and strength from her husband and father, forever held in her heart.

Visiting Eberhard always elicited memories. Eberhard Cemetery was familiar ground, only four miles from the farm, and the family's final resting place for generations. The first of Anna's family in the county, Reuben Long and Elizabeth Olinger Long, were buried close to the church. Anna's great-grandmother Catherine Hiestand Long, came to Whitley County in the late 1840s and was buried there in 1870. Anna's brother Franklin Long was buried near her parents.

On Sunday, Anna, flanked by her daughters, walked from the funeral service at Eberhard Lutheran Church to her husband's open grave in the adjacent cemetery. The west wind was brisk over the open fields across Keiser Road, and snowflakes spit periodically from a gray sky.

A familiar sight—Washington's oversized red marble tombstone— forced a smile from Anna. Dead for 18 months, he made his daughter chuckle on one of the worst days of her life. That Washington Long purchased a huge marker seemed right in character for her larger-than-life father. While his height was average, his character was colossal. No one walking to the gravesite could miss Washington Long's sizeable tombstone at the edge of Keiser Road, a towering piece of marble in three parts.

The wind whipped around the grave markers, and the funeral home tent provided little respite for the mourners. Arms still linked, Anna and her daughters stood for the brief committal service. Kellis's siblings and their children huddled behind the women, and neighbors and friends crowded around the family. Reverend N. C. McCoy of Columbia City gave the final blessing, and Kellis's casket was lowered into the ground.

Amid grief and anxiety, Anna wasn't sure how she would move forward. She and Kellis dreamed of their remaining children living on the farm, but neither daughter expressed interest. Zoe wasn't married and had a career. LeNore's husband Carl was a rising star for Prudential in Springfield, Illinois. Who would cherish the farm, now and in the future?

The legacy farm had meant survival for Anna's ancestors. Anna was born in her father's home, where he had also been born. She gave birth to her three children in her own home, on adjacent land. The farm was her means of support and her link to the pioneer past. Anna wanted her children to experience the joys and assets of the land.

For now, the Hoards' hired man could keep the fieldwork going, with Anna managing the large vegetable garden, the beehives, a dairy cow, and chickens. Those efforts did not solve the problem of the monthly loan payment. Kellis's wages from the store supplemented budget shortfalls due to low crop prices and the Depression.

As Anna and her daughters huddled at Eberhard Cemetery on a December 1932 afternoon, the farm had been in the family for 95 years. The fertile Washington Township land had sustained the family and provided security in difficult times. The Longs and their descendants worked against harsh winters, drought, disease, economic upheaval, and untimely death.

The farm was Anna's rock.

She had no intention of losing it now.

PLACE OF DEATH

County Allen

INDIANA STATE BOARD OF HEALTH
CERTIFICATE OF DEATH
(CORONERS)

Local No. 8436

Registered No.

Town
or
City Fort Wayne No. Lutheran Hospital St.
(If death occurred in a hospital or institution, give its name instead of street and number)

Length of residence in city or town where death occurred....yrs....mos....ds. How long in U. S. if of foreign birth?....yrs....mos....ds.

FULL NAME Henry Kellis Hoard

Residence: No. .... St. South Whitley, Ind.
(Usual place of abode) (If non-resident give city or town and State)

PERSONAL AND STATISTICAL PARTICULARS	CORONER'S CERTIFICATE OF DEATH
SEX Male	Color or Race White	Single Married Widowed or Divorced Married (Write the word)	DATE OF DEATH December 2 1932 (Month) (Day) (Year)

NAME OF HUSBAND or WIFE (of deceased) Anna Hoard

DATE OF BIRTH (of deceased) March 1 1870
Month Day Year

AGE 62 years 9 months 1 days

OCCUPATION
Trade, profession, or particular kind of work done, as spinner, sawyer, bookkeeper, etc. Farmer
Industry or business in which work was done, as silk mill, saw mill, bank etc.
Total time (years) spent in this occupation

BIRTHPLACE (State or country) Indiana

FATHER NAME John Hoard
BIRTHPLACE (State or country) Indiana

MOTHER MAIDEN NAME Catherine Creager
BIRTHPLACE (State or country) Indiana

I HEREBY CERTIFY, that I took charge of the remains described above, held an............thereon
(inquest, autopsy or inquiry)
and from the evidence obtained by said............
(inquest, autopsy or inquiry)
find that said deceased came to............death on the day stated above, at 5⁵⁵ A. M.

The principal cause of death and related causes of importance were as follows:
Edema of Glottis
Stricture of Oesophagus
165
Accidentally swallowed

Other contributory causes of importance:
fuming sulphuric acid
mistaken for cider

Name of operation............ Date of............
What test confirmed diagnosis? ET............ Was there an autopsy? No
(Signed) Walter E. Kruse M. D.
(Coroner or Coroner's Physician)
Dec 2, 1932 (Address) 9286 E Creighton

Burial permit issued by L. B. Keller, R.N. - Luth. Hosp. Ft. Wayne	PLACE OF BURIAL OR REMOVAL South Whitley, Ind.	DATE OF BURIAL Dec. 8 1932
Filed 12/10 1932	UNDERTAKER Miller ~ Fook	WAS THE BODY EMBALMED? Yes.
L. G. Miller Health Officer or Deputy	ADDRESS So. Whitley, Ind.	EMBALMER'S LICENSE No. 2522 + 777

1 Dreams of Moving West

FARM FOR SALE—The subscribers will offer for sale on the premises, on Saturday, the 18th, at 10 A.M., a farm on which Reuben Long now resides, containing 80 acres six miles west of Dayton on the Eaton Road. About one half is improved. There is a dwelling house on the farm and a well of good water. Also— an apple orchard through which the National Road, undoubtedly, will pass. Terms made known at the time of sale.[1]

Reuben Long set his foot into the stirrup and hoisted his muscular frame over his horse. The 35-year-old farmer was off to purchase a newspaper advertisement to sell his 80-acre Montgomery County farm at auction. Reuben clasped the reins to settle his excited mount, who was chomping at his bit, ready to go. The upbeat attitude wasn't limited to Reuben's horse. Today's trip was part of a greater design. For more than a year, Reuben had planned to move his family to Indiana, where he could buy virgin land from the federal government.

Reuben rode east on the Eaton Road to Dayton, six miles away, past his apple orchard and his extended families' farms. The summer day resonated with promise.

---

[1] "Farm for Sale (Advertisement)." The Democratic-Herald, Dayton, Ohio, June 25, 1836.

Reuben viewed his ripening crops from horseback. He saw his children playing as he rode away. He sat a little higher in the saddle, anticipating all the good things to come and enjoying the warm sun on his face.

His orchard's tree limbs would soon be pregnant with lemon-colored Maiden Blush apples, painted by Mother Nature with a red tint. A favorite of American pioneers, the hardy trees bore fruit within several years of planting.

Thirty years before, Reuben's mother, Catherine, brought the apple seeds to Ohio. Catherine loved the apple blossoms in spring and the early autumn fruit. Their delicate flowers and fragrant fruit reminded Catherine of her Virginia birthplace. When Reuben purchased his Ohio farm in the 1820s, he took a cutting from one of his mother's trees. Reuben appreciated the fullness and beauty of the orchard.

Apples from Reuben's orchard would ripen for picking in early autumn.

MAIDEN BLUSH APPLES, IMAGE PROVIDED BY FEDCO SEEDS, CLINTON ME

Reuben considered the first bite he would take on his ride into Dayton, the fruit crispy and sweet. He smiled at the thought of the pies his wife Elizabeth Olinger Long would make.

A cloudless blue sky above, Reuben surveyed with pride his farm and the farms of his parents and siblings. In three decades, what a comfortable community his parents had built. He waved at his brother John, herding sheep on his parents' farm.

John Long gave his older brother a knowing nod. John knew today was a big day for Reuben. Reuben had big dreams, much like their ancestors who came to the colonies from Prussia in 1713. When Reuben's farm sold, the brothers could move to Indiana. Reuben wanted more land in a less-populated area. To fulfill his dream, Reuben was willing to move his family hundreds of miles.

While the extended family had been expecting the move, Reuben anticipated his parents' sadness. Lewis Long and Catherine Long enjoyed having their children and grandchildren near. Reuben knew his wife, Elizabeth, would miss her parents as well.

The trip passed quickly, and soon Reuben was in Dayton. Reuben headed to *The Democratic-Herald* office to purchase an advertisement to sell his 80-acre farm. Reuben hitched his horse to a post near the center of town and walked to the newspaper.

In the city of more than 6,000 people, *The Democratic-Herald* was one of a dozen papers. Newspapers were a primary source of information in 1836. The newspaper building, a simple wooden structure, differed from ornate, neighboring architecture that featured the city's local gray limestone. Thick air emanated from gaslight fumes inside the dusty, dimly-lit room. Through grimy windows, beams of light outlined the printing press made of iron and wood.

Reuben opened the door and stepped into the dim light. He saw a nattily-dressed clerk, who was wearing a dark suit with a stiff, white cravat, gawking at him from behind a counter. In his homespun shirt and pants, Reuben wondered how the clerk stood the summer heat and humidity in his heavy clothing.

Reuben jumped into his request for an advertisement. He wanted to purchase an ad for the auction of his Eaton Road farm. Reuben told the clerk the farm had a decent well and a good house. He purchased the ad for a few cents.

Did Reuben feel a moment of regret as he walked away from the counter? He opened the door. Was he making a mistake to sell his farm? Would the future in Indiana exceed his grand expectations? While he expected the new National Road to devalue his property, what if he were wrong and land prices rose? The deed was done. The auction day was set. It was time to move ahead.

Reuben stepped outside into the bright summer day and endless possibilities.

2 Staking a Claim in Indiana

"...the elder (Reuben) Long experienced in full measure all the vicissitudes and hardships which fell to those who paved the way for civilization in the fertile lands and dense forests of northern Indiana."[2]

In November 1835, Reuben and his brother John made the first of two exploratory trips to Indiana. Through newspapers and word of mouth, the brothers learned land was selling in northeastern Indiana for half the Ohio price. Land patents were available for 40, 80, or 160 acres or more from the government office in Fort Wayne, Indiana. Settlers could stake a claim and then apply for and purchase a land patent.[3]

The brothers left for Indiana with only their horses and necessary supplies, their axes, rifles, and ammunition the most important. In the evenings, they checked the stars. They used the stars to navigate, as travelers had for centuries, seeking the North Star to determine directions. Reuben pointed out Venus, called the evening star, to his brother. The second planet from the sun was the brightest, and sometimes looked blue.

Once away from Dayton, they rarely saw another human. Guns at their side, the brothers watched for wild animals, both for their safety and for dinner. Northwest Ohio and Northeast Indiana were still forested and wild. The brothers occasionally met other white settlers and indigenous peoples. The farther north from Dayton the brothers traveled, the more challenging conditions became.

---

[2] Kaler, Samuel P., and Richard H. Maring. The History of Whitley County, Indiana. Indianapolis, Indiana: B.F. Bowen & Co., 1907. P. 580.

[3] A land patent differs from homesteading. With homesteading, the government gives away the land. A land patent is similar to a deed for acreage purchased from the federal government.

Bare branches and less undergrowth provided the men with a good line of sight. An unobstructed view was perhaps the only advantage of winter travel, assuming no rain, sleet, or snow. Precipitation of all forms slowed the brothers to a crawl. They shivered even in thick coonskin caps, buckskin coats, and breeches, which did not keep them entirely warm.

Turning west near the St. Mary's River, John and Reuben followed the river on the south side until reaching Indiana.

The brothers could hear the roaring of an unnamed river from a mile away. The rushing water dotted with pieces of ice sloshed above its banks. Its depth was a mystery. Would the horses swim? The brothers planned another route if the gyrating, frigid water was too deep. Reuben gave John his reins and stepped out into the river to see if he could assess its depth. At the mid-point, the water didn't go over his knees. It was wickedly fast. Reuben and John rode their horses across the river.

Reuben needed to dry off his feet and legs, and ward off frostbite. John lighted a fire. The horse blankets had stayed dry enough to gradually warm Reuben's feet and toes.

Back in the saddle, the men headed west of the river. The brothers had hacked their way through many Ohio forests, but nothing like this wall of colossal trees ahead in Indiana. Massive, soaring trees—oak, maple, and walnut—guarded the virgin wood like primordial sentries. These were once-in-a-lifetime trees, a result of centuries of undisturbed hardwood growth. Against a pale blue winter sky, the bare tree branches reached up like a thousand empty hands, seeking warmth from the sun.

For Reuben and John, while the forest was beautiful, getting through it was a challenge. They used their axes and rifles every day, hacking through the woods and hunting for food. The men enjoyed swinging their axes—the exercise upped their body temperatures. While their progress was slow, the brothers made better time on horseback than fellow pioneers whose wagons took a beating with each rut and hole.

꙳

A few weeks after leaving Dayton, Reuben and John arrived in Whitley County, Indiana, about 60 miles west of the Ohio state line. This unfamiliar land was where Reuben staked his claim, with John's claim marked a few miles away on the following day. The brothers inspected a swampy area dotted by boulders. Surrounded by acres and acres of trees, the men studied what would become Reuben's farm.

Could this undeveloped and marshy land stretched before them become Reuben's paradise? Reuben didn't see the downside in the frozen swamps and forests in their first moments on his claim. He saw an opportunity. This land was where the brothers would each begin new lives. The brothers had experienced weeks of hardships for this dream, traveling through icy waters, and dense, uncut forests, from Dayton to Whitley County, a trip of more than 150 miles on horseback.

Reuben pulled a wooden stake out of his saddle pack. He pounded the stake into the hard ground, leaving half above to mark his stake. It was an impetuous act; Reuben claimed the land with no legal documentation, only a willingness to work hard and make it his paradise. As the light faded from the day, John and Reuben broke out in huge smiles, and John slapped his big brother on the back.

Pounding the wooden stake into the ground was a symbol for the brothers, a small task they repeated the next day on John's stake. This land, undrained and wild as it was, held their hopes and dreams and would eventually be home for their growing families. The men made a fire and camped for the first time in Indiana, exhausted from travel, but exhilarated over their new ventures.

The Long brothers chopped down enough trees to build small, rudimentary cabins and squatted on the land. They collected stones for their fireplaces. Snow melt provided water as did a stream, later named Sugar Creek, that ran through Reuben's future farm.

Reuben's application for 160 acres in Washington Township was recorded at the Fort Wayne Land Patent Office on February 7, 1836. John's application was noted shortly after, both likely recorded on their return to Dayton.[4] The price was right. It was a bargain at $1.25 per acre, half the price of land in southwestern Ohio.

---

[4] The United States of America by Martin Van Buren, President, to Reuben Long, Patent Deed dated August 1, 1837, recorded February 7, 1836, Deed record 80, page 594, certification number 9932.

Amy McVay Abbott

3 Swamp Township

Reuben's 80-acre Ohio farm sold at auction on August 18, 1836. There was no turning back.

Reuben and his brother readied for a second trip to northeastern Indiana shortly after the farm sold. This time, they would travel with a team of horses and a wagon loaded with tools and supplies. Elizabeth Olinger Long packed several cast-iron pans, blankets, and large cloth bags, which, when stuffed with straw or at worst, pine needles, served as beds. Elizabeth added touches of home, an extra pair of breeches, lye soap, and hardtack, a chewy cracker that did not spoil. If everything went well, Reuben, Elizabeth, their children, and John, his wife Mary, and son Perry, would move permanently to Indiana the following spring.

And while the men desperately needed a team of oxen to help in clearing land, oxen would have slowed the trip to a crawl through the dense forests. Purchasing a team of the horned beasts would have to wait until the permanent move.

Having traveled to Whitley County the year before, Reuben and John knew what challenges lay ahead. The men tied extra wooden wheels onto the wagon for good measure, expecting rugged paths. Old trails had, in some places, turned into roads. Much of their travel was simply a gamble, depending on the season and rain. If they got lucky, they might run across new paths other settlers carved out.

Still, Reuben anticipated a more comfortable trip this time with a wagon to sleep in and early autumn weather. The paths were wet in winter, muddy in spring and late fall. But early autumn may have been the best time to go. They were leaving two months earlier than the prior year. The severe rains usually came in November; the brothers were traveling in early September.

The brothers headed north from Dayton, again turning west toward Indiana. Reuben tensed as they approached the scene of their rough river cross the year before. The riverbed was easily crossed, with neither brother bounced from the buckboard nor receiving a baptismal dunking in the muddy water.

In Indiana, early autumn overgrowth of the dense forests somewhat hindered travel. Reuben and John swung their axes, whacking tangled vines. A canopy of colorful leaves overhead filtered sunlight, slowing travel in their last hours before reaching their stakes. They took turns leading the team and wagon, while the other chopped his way through the forest.

In the late afternoon, Reuben and John reached a small clearing on Reuben's 1835 stake. A creek later named Sugar Creek rippled ahead in the late afternoon sunlight. How relieved the brothers were to be on familiar ground after a long journey from Dayton. How good they felt about being back in Indiana.

The cabin the brothers had built the previous year was on the other side of Sugar Creek. Eager to reach his cabin, Reuben slapped the reins, and the horses pulled the wagon and its drivers up a slight rise.

But Reuben's cabin wasn't there.

Where Reuben's new home had been, nothing stood but a scattering of stones and the outline of where the cabin had been.

No logs bound neatly together, no mud chinks and stone chimney, no framed doorway. The brothers looked around. Maybe they had gotten lost and weren't at the right place. No, Sugar Creek anchored the location. All their hard work in the cold and winter had disappeared.[5]

What in the world had happened here? The brothers had built a small cabin on each stake on their 1835 trip. Would John's place have been burned as well?

The Long brothers were bewildered and disheartened. Up in smoke. Could it have been a lightning strike? They had encountered no trouble with the few white settlers they met on their first visit. And the few

---

[5] Indiana Historical Society, "Application for Centennial Farm Family Seal" Submitted by Berniece Long Piepho and Carl and LeNore Enz, Indianapolis 4, Indiana: 140 N. Senate Avenue, 1947.

members of the Miami or the Potawatomi tribes who wandered through occasionally were friendly and spoke a few English words. Reuben saw Indians bowhunting deer in the woods during the 1835 early-1836 visit.

Reuben and John knew several hundred natives lived in the county, primarily at Seeks Village in Columbia Township and scattered encampments along the Eel River. Rumors abounded at trading posts—the brothers had heard stories of burned cabins on the Columbia Township line.

The brothers were furious and exhausted. Reuben and John made a fire as the sun set. They camped as they had every night for three weeks. Their adventuresome spirit had them awake early the next morning, felling trees for a new cabin.

Reuben learned from the Miami themselves that they had burned his cabin.[6] The reason why is unclear. However, the natives and the brothers worked together to rebuild Reuben's home. The help of the Miami in felling trees for Reuben's rebuilt cabin had been a lifesaver.

❧

Reuben knew a burned cabin was probably the least of his worries about the difficulties of pioneer life. The swamp itself, few neighbors, and reptiles presented other concerns.

Settlers nicknamed the boggy, wet area Swamp Township. The marshy land served as a breeding ground for mosquitoes and the deadly diseases that accompanied bug-ridden swamps. Mosquitoes carrying malaria thrived in the wetlands.

The brothers lacked a team of oxen. When they began farming, Reuben and John would need fields free of tree stumps. Reuben could chop down trees with his ax, but stump removal required the steady pull of a team of 1200-pound oxen. Instead, the brothers dug around the stump until enough could be chopped away, which often left huge holes. Farmers filled the holes with dirt, but the first good rain washed the soil away. This method explained why, for several decades, Indiana fields were dotted with tree stumps. Improvements to drainage would take decades.

Without someone watching their cabins, the brothers were wary of traveling to purchase a team of oxen or much else. Settlers in 1835 and

---

[6] Written notes by Berniece Long Piepho, found with Indiana Historical Society application, see footnote 5.

1836 generally traveled to the livestock market in Elkhart or Wabash, cities that also had a mill and stores. A trip meant an absence from their stakes for a week to 10 days. That wasn't a good option, based on the history of Reuben's first cabin. Neither man would get a team until returning with their families.

The woods also contained daily dangers. Predatory coyotes and wolves owned the forests, especially at night. Of more significant concern were the poisonous water moccasins in the swamps. Reuben worried about the snakes that could kill a man in one bite and spied rattlesnakes everywhere, in forests, under rocks, near cabins. Ironically, a rattlesnake indigenous to northern Indiana was called the Massanutten rattlesnake, an ironic nod to the town Reuben's great-grandfather helped found in Virginia.

Reuben had some wonderful features on his land, access to water, and plenty of wild game for hunting on the positive side of the ledger.

Reuben's acreage featured bountiful Sugar Creek, a small stream that opened the world beyond. Sugar Creek flowed into the nearby Eel River. A person could travel from Whitley County to the Gulf of Mexico from Sugar Creek. Pioneers could take the Eel River southwest to the Wabash River, then south to the Ohio River. The broad Ohio joined the even-wider and grander Mississippi River, all the way to New Orleans, and on to the Gulf of Mexico.

While there is no record of the men digging a well or finding a spring, water was an absolute necessity. Sugar Creek may have been spring-fed, providing a clean source of water.

Any settler who could use a bow or a gun did not go hungry, with the abundance of wild turkey and pheasants, and of course, the ubiquitous white-tailed deer. Venison was a staple of the brothers' diet and added the bonus of buckskin for coats and shoes.

The dangers of extreme weather, disease, and wild animals were offset by the land's potential, access to water, and the plethora of wild game. With sound drainage systems later added, Swamp Township residents would ultimately farm some of the richest soil for raising crops in Indiana. Windmills would soon dot rural Whitley County, their wind-fueled pumps easing water collection.

4 The Old Country

Reuben's average physical appearance belied his stout constitution. Perhaps his character was inherited from his ancestors who came to colonial America in the early 1700s from Prussia. Philip Lung and Kathryn von Zerfass Lung, Reuben's great-grandparents, immigrated through Philadelphia in 1713, settling in Lancaster County, Pennsylvania. Many Prussians came to the colonies, aggravated with high taxes and strict inheritance laws.

Philip changed their surname from Lung to Long. Kathryn's maiden name had been von Zerfass, changed to Surface. Kathryn's father, a European noble, was born in 1650 in Koblenz, Rheinland-Pfalz. Count Kurt von Zerfass married an English bride, Lady Jody Bartholemew, about 1684.

Primarily of English birth, citizens of Philadelphia weren't enamored hearing German spoken on their streets. Five ships arrived at the Port of Philadelphia in one month, bringing 300 immigrants from the German states.[7] Unfortunately, the anti-immigrant attitude wasn't limited to the cities.

Philip Long and his wife Katherine didn't stay in Philadelphia but settled in Lancaster County, Pennsylvania. Many immigrants from their region settled in Lancaster County, calling themselves the "Pennsylvania Dutch," an adaptation of the word "Deutsch" from their homeland.

---

[7] Woodward, Virginia. "German Immigration to Pennsylvania in the Early 1700s - Lynn-Heidelberg Historical Society." Accessed February 5, 2021. http://www.lynnheidelberg.org/beginnewlife.html, undated.

In 1729, Philip bought 800 acres in Virginia's Shenandoah Valley from frontier land speculator Jacob Stover, an ancestor of President Dwight D. Eisenhower.[8]

Thirteen men, including Philip, and his son, Paul Long, purchased nearly 5,000 acres in the Massanutten area but did not immediately receive land deeds. The group petitioned colonial Governor William Gooch for clear titles in 1733.

On December 15, 1733, the colonial courts gave Stover his land grants. The petitioners, including Philip and Paul, received their property deed for 800 acres. The Longs became well-known and prosperous farmers in the Shenandoah Valley.

Many of the Prussian immigrants were Catholic. Some were Lutheran and Mennonite, a faith also called Dunkard or Brethren. Colonial Lutherans sometimes partnered with the Dunkards and embraced their anti-war stance. The early Longs stayed faithful to their Lutheran and Mennonite roots. They taught their children Luther's *Small Catechism* and tenets of their faith.[9]

MONUMENT TO FOUNDERS OF MASSANUTTEN, VIRGINIA, IN THE SHENANDOAH VALLEY INCLUDE PHILIP LONG, SR. AND HIS SON PAUL LONG. IMAGE SOURCE: A SHORT HISTORY OF MASSANUTTEN, VIRGINIA.

German cultural traditions would survive for generations. As had their mothers, women made traditional lebkuchen loaves. Some loaves were sweet, others spicy, many featured large amounts of honey. Whether German immigrants' affinity for honey drove them to keep bees or keeping bees drove them to use it in bread is a chicken-and-egg question.

Prussians were also fond of beer. A local farmer generally grew barley and hops and brewed a good stout beer for friends and family.

Prussia was the source of many American Christmas traditions. Children placed lighted candles and berries on a cut pine or spruce tree, a tradition going back to Martin Luther's time. While English was the accepted first language, many churches held services and sang liturgy and songs in German until the 20th century. Many immigrants continued speaking their familiar German language at home or church. During worship services, women and small children typically sat on one side of the

---

8 "Philip Long (1678-1755) - Find A Grave Memorial." Find a Grave. Accessed February 5, 2021. https://www.findagrave.com/memorial/50213963/philip-long.
9 Wayland, John. "A History of Shenandoah County". Strasburg, Virginia: Shenandoah Publishing House, 1927, page 90.

congregation, while men sat on the other. The greater community, however, frowned on other languages spoken besides English. Most colonists learned the language.

Until the middle of the 18th century, the colonists lived in peace with the indigenous peoples. Around 1750, white settlers began to outnumber the indigenous peoples, and uprisings began. Reuben's uncle Philip (grandson of the original Philip) built Fort Philip Long, a 900-acre complex recognized by the National Historic Register of Buildings in 1973. Philip Long, Junior, built a limestone house and buildings on the Shenandoah riverbank, a fortress to ward off attacks. Treaties with various tribes usurped land used by indigenous people for centuries. The federal government forced tribes to move west; however, many native peoples still lived in 18th-century Virginia.

⁂

African slaves first arrived at Jamestown, Virginia, in 1619, starting the American legacy of bondage to white families. Planters in coastal Virginia were the first to use enslaved Africans in labor-intensive tobacco production. The crop had an eleven-month cycle from planting to harvest, subjecting those who were enslaved on a tobacco plantation to the most challenging conditions.

Philip Long, Senior, and his children, including Henry Long, were slave owners. Both owned plantations with significant acreage and likely owned a large number of enslaved people.

Due to the terrain and altitude, the Longs did not grow tobacco in the Shenandoah region. They raised animals, grain crops, and vegetables. Most plantation owners

HENRY LONG SERVED AS A PRIVATE IN THE VIRGINIA REGIMENT DURING THE REVOLUTIONARY WAR. FAMILY DOCUMENT. WAR DEPARTMENT COLLECTION OF REVOLUTIONARY WAR RECORDS, RG 93; NATIONAL ARCHIVES, WASHINGTON DC.

treated the enslaved people poorly, providing crude cabins on their property, often splitting families, and working their slaves from sunup to sundown. Before McCormack's reaper brought automation to farming, landowners like Philip and Henry assigned the enslaved people to the farm's dirtiest, most back-breaking jobs. The enslaved people had a few hours on Sundays and Christmas off, which they used to care for their own families and homes.

On the backs of people of color, the Longs and other white settlers became more affluent in the colonies. The Long family espoused a faith of peace and tolerance. Yet, Philip and Henry owned other human beings. White landowners passed land and slaves—fellow human beings they did not value more than a tool—onto the next generation. Reuben's grandfather, Henry Long, son of Philip, owned about 500 acres in the Shenandoah Valley. When his will was written later in his life, he had sold most of his land and slaves. In a portion of Henry's 1779 will, he bequeathed an enslaved person to his wife in the same sentence as he gave her a saddle.

> Item, I give and bequeath to my well-beloved wife my Negro man and home and saddle, and the rest I remand the manner plantation and the third of my stock during of her widowship.[10]

While the Prussian immigrants experienced the English citizens' wrath and bigotry, they saw no problem emulating the English slave-owning behavior. The horror of African-American enslavement would not be corrected for 150 years. And systemic racism has not yet been overcome, a stain on the family and the American story.

A mystery is why the pacifist Henry Long enlisted in the Continental Army late in his life. He died almost immediately upon finishing his service in the Virginia Infantry.

Many Prussian immigrants kept moving west in search of undeveloped land. Many sought land with hardwood trees they could clear, both for farming and for timber. Where hardwood trees grew, the immigrants believed the soil was rich and fertile.

Philip Long and his wife left Pennsylvania for Virginia, and their grandson, Lewis, son of Henry, would eventually leave Virginia for Ohio. Lewis's son Reuben was born in 1801 in Virginia.

---

[10] Ancestry.com, *Virginia U.S. Land, Marriage, and Probate Records, 1639-1850* [Database online], Provo, Utah, USA: Ancestry.com Operations Inc., 2004.

Lewis and his wife, Catherine Hiestand Long, left Virginia after Reuben's birth, likely with a cash share from Henry's estate. History doesn't reveal if Lewis Long left the slave state on principle or wanderlust. His son Isaac's birth was recorded in Montgomery County in May 1806. Lewis remained a farmer, a tradition that would direct family choices for the Long family's future generations.

America was growing into a large nation. By the end of the 19th century, it would cover all ground from the Atlantic to the Pacific—by frontiersmen, entrepreneurs, and a few scoundrels—in this new patchwork quilt of a nation.

Amy McVay Abbott

5 Friendship Born of Necessity

A nearly instant kinship and camaraderie developed between southwestern Ohio citizens who came to Whitley County. Neighbors, or groups who shared religious faith, often emigrated together. Like Reuben and John Long, men often came first to find land and build a cabin, leaving wives and children in Ohio.

By August 1, 1837, when Reuben and John's land patents were approved, many white settlers had already brought families to Whitley County. Reuben and John struck out on their first two trips to Indiana alone.

In 1836, Samuel Obenchain and Catharine Flora Obenchain settled on 160 acres in Cleveland Township, Whitley County. Their nearest neighbor, James Abbott, lived five miles west in Kosciusko County among the early settlers. With only their horses and wagon, they arrived with little and traveled to Elkhart County to purchase

US Department of the Interior, Bureau of Land Management, State volume patent, Indiana, document #9932, issued August 1, 1837.

livestock and supplies. The Obenchains are believed to be the first permanent white settlers in Cleveland Township. Samuel was a candidate for judge in 1836 and lost to Jesse Cleveland, for whom the township is named. Had Obenchain won, would it be Obenchain Township today?

In 1839, Obenchain purchased four lots within the city limits of South Whitley.[11]

- With a stash of gold coins in his handkerchief, Jonas Baker arrived in Washington Township sometime in the mid-1830s. He walked native American-style, barefoot, from Stark County, Ohio, to Indiana, with only his gold, the clothes on his back, and an ax. Baker first paid property taxes on a 160-acre farm in the southeastern end of Washington Township, assessed in 1841 for the prior year.[12] Shortly after, he bought another 160 acres adjacent to his first purchase. His unorthodox arrival earned Baker a reputation among local gossips. For the rest of his life, Baker supplied the chin waggers with hijinks and bad behavior. Occasionally, the wealthy farmer offered an act of kindness, with the receiver unaware. However, Jonas was a hard worker who cleared out his farm with little assistance before starting his own family in 1843 when he married Mariah Haines in Montgomery County, Ohio, and brought her back to Whitley County.
- Peter Creager, Senior, and wife Elizabeth Rike Creager, neighbors of the Longs from Dayton, moved to a 160-acre farm a few miles west of Reuben's stake and near the Obenchains.

Over time, the children of original Whitley County families would marry. Four families—the Longs, the Obenchains, the Creagers, and the Bakers—would ultimately become interconnected, an accident of time and place. Their children and grandchildren would build their own families and sense of community, some blessed, some cursed.

---

[11] Weston Arthur Goodspeed and Charles Blanchard, "Counties of Whitley and Noble, Indiana, Historical and Biographical," Massachusetts: Higginson Book Co., 1992, p. 297.

[12] Thompson, Meredith. "1841 Tax Rolls of Washington Township, Whitley County, Indiana," Indiana Genealogical Society - Main Page. Indiana Genealogical Society. Accessed February 5, 2021. http://www.indgensoc.org/.

6 Rattlesnakes, Wolves, and Wildflowers

Peter Creager, Senior, perched on the wagon seat beside his wife, Elizabeth, and motioned for a second wagon to follow him. Peter and Elizabeth, and their children Adam, Christian Henry, Levi, Peter Junior, John, and Lydia left Montgomery County, Ohio, on October 26, 1836, for Indiana. They brought a supply of garden seeds including apple and peach seeds from their Dayton orchards, four extra horses, five head of cattle, six hogs, three dogs, and a tent. One son, Ezra, and his wife Delilah Creager decided to stay in Preble County, Ohio.

While some settlers like the Longs made preparatory trips to the Northwest Territories ahead of moving, others like the Creagers moved without ever seeing their new land. The Creagers packed everything and moved to Whitley County, lock, stock, and barrel.

For more than three weeks, the Creager family rode north through west-central Ohio and turned west towards Indiana, following the same route as the Longs. The horses struggled to pull the overloaded wagons on trails sticky with mud, snow, and ice. A wagon became impossibly stuck, only 20 miles from their new home. Peter sent his son Christian Creager out on horseback for help. At 15, Christian was reliable and already skilled with a rifle and hunting knife. What could go wrong?

Christian rode off into the Huntington County wilderness. The family unloaded the goods from the broken wagon and packed the remaining wagon with a heavy load. With Christian still not having returned, the family set up camp for the night.

Christian found no help and spent a cold night with only his horse and his rifle. Having failed to bring a flintstone, Christian had no fire and could not see in the dark woods to find something to flash on a stone. He slept on the ground in two inches of snow. Christian caught up with his worried family after dawn but brought no assistance. Later that afternoon, the family arrived in Whitley County, November 15, with one overloaded wagon and a team, five sons on weighted-down horses with two riderless, and a worn-out family, ready for a warm fire and rest.

Peter bought a 160-acre farm in Cleveland Township through the federal Land Patent Office. Cleveland Township is west of Washington Township in Whitley County. His documentation had not arrived before he left his Dayton home, but he knew the location and discerned his land was a few miles south of the Eel River in southern Cleveland Township.

> "The night before we landed in the township, some Indians killed a male member of their tribe. They dug a hole big enough to bury him standing straight up, with his head sticking out," Christian told a historian in 1902.[13]

> Around him, they built a log pen and placed his rifle, tomahawk, butcher knife, and a bottle of whiskey inside the enclosure around the man's head.

> These items didn't remain long with their late master. Still, the body remained there and decayed until the head fell off. Dr. Joseph Hayes, of Collamer, reportedly picked up the dead man's head while passing through.[14] Hayes' son gave the head to a Pierceton doctor. Christian would tell this tale and others throughout his life.

Having five sons was a huge advantage for the Creagers because neighbors were scarce for cabin-raising at the end of 1836. The Creagers were among the first dozen families in their part of Whitley County. Building a cabin, especially under the pressure of winter, was an arduous task. Peter and his sons immediately cut down several large trees and dragged them to their cabin site. Settlers cleared land around their cabins to spot predators in the open.

Trees grew in abundance; however, the Creagers were particular about which ones they chose for their cabin. They needed good straight trees to make logs for the cabin sides and clapboard, thinner pieces for a roof. With six men to fell and lift timber, the cabin could be a story-and-a-half, with a clapboard floor in the sleeping area.

---

[13] Kaler, Samuel P., and Richard H. Maring, "History of Whitley County, Indiana," Indianapolis, Indiana, B.F. Bowen & Co., 1907, p. 122.
[14] Kaler, Samuel P., and Richard H. Maring, "History of Whitley County, Indiana," Indianapolis, Indiana: B.F. Bowen & Co., 1907, p. 123.

The family assembled all four walls with logs notched to another and stacked. The younger children filled gaps between the logs with clay, mud, and smaller pieces of wood, a process known as daubing or chinking. The men cut out the door and holed out space for a fireplace on another side. A south-facing door allowed the sun to shine in the cabin when open during the day. The door was also made of timber, with a wooden latch and a buckskin string. Settlers placed large flat rocks under the four corners to level the house.

The fireplace, built of rocks and mud, was large enough to stack wood three or four feet high; keeping the fire ablaze was essential for warmth and cooking. Elizabeth Creager and her older girls tended the fire.

ELIZABETH RIKE CREAGER,
WIFE OF PETER CREAGER, SR.
FAMILY IMAGE.

The Creagers moved out of the overcrowded tent and into their 22-foot square cabin on Christmas Day 1836. They settled a few miles west of former Dayton neighbors Reuben Long and John Long in Washington Township, though neither knew it immediately. Reuben and John would not settle permanently for several years.

Forests in both townships were primarily unbroken. The Creagers soon cut paths to Springfield, quickly renamed South Whitley, where about a dozen families already settled.

Moving in winter meant bringing enough supplies to feed the large family. The menfolk hunted and kept the larder full of wild game. Deer grazed with the Creagers' cattle, and the family had plenty of venison. Elizabeth cured deer meat to make jerky, a staple of their diet and a snack for supply trips.

Several of the older boys filled their packs with jerky and traveled 40 miles to Marion. The boys purchased breadstuffs such as flour and cornmeal at a Missisinewa River water mill on this multi-day wagon trip.

The family cleared eight acres in time to plant corn and a vegetable garden during the spring of 1837. The rattlesnakes were thick that year. The Creager boys competed to catch and kill the snakes. A neighbor in Cleveland Township killed 28 snakes that spring. Ridding the area of venomous snakes was appreciated by all, and snakeskin made suitable belts. Along with the abundance of wild game, corn and vegetables held them through 1837 and into the terrible year of 1838.

The ubiquitous white-tailed deer was a godsend when the Creagers' cows drank water containing leeches and got sick with bloody murrain,[15] causing a loss of 28 cows in their first few years in Indiana. Pioneers fed corn to domestic hogs, giving them a source for bacon and ham. Wild hogs were also plentiful and not to be messed with by a curious child. Wild hogs could do severe damage to a human or animal.[16]

Even as teenagers, the Creager sons were skilled woodsmen and used rifles for hunting and protection. Their new home offered almost daily dangers, and at the least, different adventures than they had known in the more populated Dayton region.

Christian's father asked him to deliver fresh pork to Christian's brother-in-law John Cunningham. In the late afternoon, Christian mounted his horse for the four-mile ride to the Cunningham's cabin as the sun dipped below the treetops.

He had no trouble finding his way, but darkness surrounded him before he reached the cabin. Wolves, smelling the fresh meat, followed Christian, their yellow eyes flashing in the dark all around him.

His gun was still at his side. The wolves were thicker now, with their ever-closer chorus of mournful cries. Christian was safe on his horse. For the moment, the creatures dared not risk a kick from its hooves or a bite from the horse's enormous teeth.

He rode to the cabin and tied his horse to the corner. Christian hurried the meat into the house, but the wolves followed him, stopping at the door but howling loudly around the house. Cunningham turned his three dogs outside, hoping the canines would chase away their ancient cousins. An eerie calm and quiet settled over the cabin. Then, banging hard against the cabin door, the dogs rammed into the room, falling over each other, and damaging the wooden door latch. The dogs could only stave off the hungry wolves for so long, and then needed their rescue, crashing into the house and startling the settlers.

The Cunninghams and their impromptu guest may have had a sleepless night, as the wolves howled until near dawn and then retreated into the

---

[15] Kaler, Samuel P., and Richard H. Maring, "History of Whitley County, Indiana," Indianapolis, Indiana: B.F. Bowen & Co., 1907, p. 122.
[16] "Hoosiers and the American Story," page 60, Indiana Historical Society Press, by Jane Hedeen, 2015.

dense woods. Like the lurking wolves, danger was always present for the pioneers in ways modern citizens cannot fathom. The settlers, not the predatory animals, were the newcomers, usurping wild and free land. Man versus nature was an entirely new situation for the animals. In the 1840s in rural Indiana, it was anyone's guess who would triumph.

7 Making a Home in the Wilderness

A person once said if Christ came back to earth in the 1830s, He would have been familiar with farming methods. The scythe, flail, and wooden plow would have been common. Oxen would have been used to plow the new ground. Oxen were much stronger and steadier on the plow than horses.[17]

When Reuben and John Long returned to Dayton in early 1837, they planned to move their families to Indiana the following summer or fall. For whatever reason—perhaps the birth of daughter Sarah Long in October 1837—the families didn't move to Whitley County until early spring 1838.

Early the next year, the families moved permanently to their new farms in Whitley County. With their children Jacob, Catherine, and baby Sarah, Reuben and Elizabeth Long settled into the log cabin that replaced the original one burned by the Miami tribe. John and Mary Long moved into their nearby cabin with their son, Perry.

Before moving, Elizabeth Long relied on her husband's tales of his trips to their new home. Both Elizabeth and Reuben fully understood the difficulties of pioneer life. Her parents, Jacob Olinger, and Maria Olinger of Pennsylvania moved to Ohio in the early 19th century when Elizabeth was a child. After Maria's 1840 death, Jacob Olinger would follow his daughter to Whitley County.

Elizabeth soon discovered life was much more than Reuben's stories of native peoples, wolves, and overgrown forests. The spring of 1838 brought unimaginable problems for a family settling for the first time. Torrential rains started in the spring and kept the ground wet. Rain

---

[17] McVay, William G. "History of the Long Hoard Enz McVay Farm in Washington Township, Whitley County, Indiana." West Lafayette, Indiana, 2010.

showers poured daily until the middle of June, when the family could finally start planting. Some wheat never germinated because of the heat.[18]

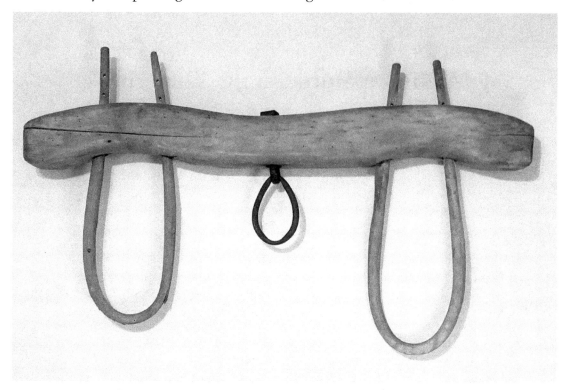

REUBEN LONG BROUGHT HIS OXEN YOKE FROM OHIO TO HIS NEW FARM IN WHITLEY COUNTY.
IMAGE PROVIDED BY ANDREW MCVAY.

There was no more rain until the end of fall. The swamps, which had filled during the rains, now lost water levels due to the intense summer heat. Marshy land filled with mosquitoes, and the mosquitoes spread malaria throughout the area. Fortunately, no family members died. However, the family did not get the jumpstart on their farm and expected a meager harvest.[19]

&

The Longs made friends quickly, out of necessity. Without a good neighbor with an ax or knowledge about finding a spring, many families

[18] Weston Arthur Goodspeed and Charles Blanchard, "Counties of Whitley and Noble, Indiana, Historical and Biographical," Salem, Massachusetts: Higginson Book Co., 1992, p. 467.
[19] Kaler, Samuel P., and Richard H. Maring, "History of Whitley County, Indiana," Indianapolis, Indiana: B.F. Bowen & Co., 1907, p. 181.

got into trouble. Without shelter, survival was questionable. Without water, survival was impossible.

By the following season, Reuben and John had each purchased an oxen team, which significantly upped productivity. Reuben and his oldest son, Jacob, cleared land with his oxen team. His team wore the wooden yoke Reuben brought from Ohio. The power of a team of 1200-pound animals made removing stumps easier; cutting, digging, and dragging had been a back-breaking process. The yoked animals gave rise to another way to subsidize the farm income—selling timber—which would last through the 19th century. A victim of progress, the massive thousand-year-old forest was nearly gone by the end of the century.

By late spring 1839, Reuben and John each helped the other plant corn in fields cleared by the oxen. One man dug a hole, while the other dropped three or four seeds before covering them with soil. Settlers could plant about an acre of corn a day, in rows as the natives had for centuries. By the time the corn grew knee-high in rows, surrounding woods and Sugar Creek's bank were carpeted with mid-summer wildflowers—from the fragrant heliotrope to red and yellow geraniums and blankets of yellow buttercup. While Sugar Creek didn't provide a wide array of fish, Mother Nature covered the banks each summer with wild onions, excellent for flavoring food.

Where sunlight and shadow merged grew eight-inch-high yellow violets with tiny, delicate blooms. Tall Solomon's Seal, stalks of green with pairs of creamy white flowers, covered the forest floor.

Reuben's daughter Catherine helped the family by digging holes and planting potatoes and pumpkins near tree stumps not yet cleared away. A child could eliminate the jimson weed, velvetleaf, and thistles between the cornrows with a hoe. With unfettered growth, both the oval-leafed jimson weed, and smooth velvetleaf could grow taller than the children. The thistle was the first weed attacked by children, who feared its spiny punctures as it grew larger. Learning how to use a hoe was a valuable skill for a pioneer child. Who knew when an errant snake would cross a child's path and need to be chopped in half? For a rattler or a large snake, children ran to get an adult and got out of the way. But the common rat snake was fair game for even the smallest child with a hoe.

Most pioneer wives and children planted vegetable and flower gardens. The white-tailed deer enjoyed crashing the garden party. Settlers built more substantial wood-post fences inside the property's split-rail fences. The animal could jump both fences, and dine on fresh vegetables, including sweet potatoes, squash, carrots, cabbage, lettuce, and onions. The Long children tried to stay ahead of the foragers, monitoring the produce daily and picking as soon as plants ripened. Elizabeth canned vegetables, burying them in the ground or a dug-out root cellar for winter consumption.

Reuben and John, with the help of neighbors, each built a barn. In the autumn, the corn was harvested, vegetables and fruit picked, again by hand. What a family grew could sustain them for a year or two.

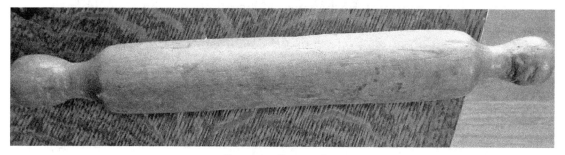

ELIZABETH OLINGER LONG BROUGHT HER ROLLING PIN FROM OHIO TO HER NEW HOME IN THE LATE 1930S. OBJECT OWNED BY AUTHOR.

The harvested corn dried in the barn away from hungry wild animals. The family used a simple grinder to make coarse cornmeal, the basis for many meals Elizabeth made her family. Corn pone was a flatbread with the corn mixture and water fried in a flat skillet. Corn mush resembled porridge. Many pioneer children loved johnnycake, a pancake made from cornmeal. With the ready availability of fresh meat, most Whitley County families did not go hungry, hanging salted or preserved meat in the barn or a root cellar.

Harvest ended the annual cycle, a time for celebration. But settlers never rested on their laurels. Farm life had adversity built into its hard-scrabble process, the sole benefit often being survival.

Indiana had been admitted to the United States by the time the 1830 nationwide census was taken. The further substantial growth of over 500 percent in a decade took the total number of 1840 residents to 147,178.[20]

---

[20] "Indiana Population 2021," Indiana Population 2021 (Demographics, Maps, Graphs). Accessed February 5, 2021.
https://worldpopulationreview.com/states/indiana-population.

8 Visiting Turkey Lake

Christian Creager rode on horseback beside his father, Peter, on a 25-mile supply trip to Closson's Mill in Syracuse. Going on the journey alone with his father was a treat. Christian usually jostled with his siblings for his father's attention.

After riding for a couple of days, Peter and Christian reached Turkey Lake, later called Wawasee, south of Syracuse. Stretched before them was a large freshwater lake, unlike anything Christian had ever seen. At least a mile across and several miles long, the lake had multiple inlets slicing into forests. Christian, a storyteller all his life, memorized special moments to tell his siblings and, ultimately, children and grandchildren. He would not forget his first view of Turkey Lake for the rest of his life.[21]

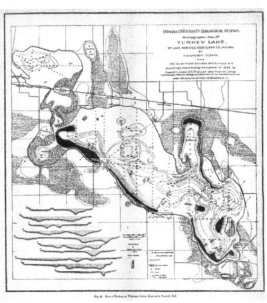

MAP OF TURKEY LAKE, WELLS LIBRARY MAP COLLECTION, INDIANA UNIVERSITY, BLOOMINGTON, INDIANA.

In Syracuse, the men shopped for needed items on the farm for several days and purchased the needed flour from Closson's Mill. Their horses loaded with supplies for their return, Peter and Christian encountered about 150 Indians near the south end of Turkey Lake. A few natives

---

[21] Kaler, Samuel P., and Richard H. Maring. "History of Whitley County," Indiana. Indianapolis, Indiana: B.F. Bowen & Co., 1907.

stopped Peter and Christian. Neither of the Creagers knew a word of the Algonquin language spoken by the tribes of northeastern Indiana.[22]

The tribesmen were friendly and motioned for the men to follow. Peter and Christian trailed them around the lake to their encampment. A massive fire was burning, with kettles suspended on poles over the flames. Native women supervised cooking the next meal, meat hunted by the men, and vegetables and greens gathered by the children.

Peter and Christian surveyed the camp. Peter spied a large ash tree log with a slab cut out. Christian pried the top with his ax and found a dead baby inside. Peter and Christian knew burial customs varied among the tribes. Some buried bodies in the ground, horizontally or vertically. Burial rites were steeped in tradition, different for every region.

Through gestures, Peter and Christian learned the papoose died recently. The log coffin served as a sacred place for the mourning family until the baby was buried.

The Indians invited Peter and Christian to eat a meal and spend the night, but father and son moved south despite the offer for a warm fire and dinner. They camped for the night, pulling supplies from their packs. Christian made a fire, this time remembering a flint. Travel by horseback was slow, but in a few days, the men arrived home, greeted by Elizabeth and the family. Christian had tales to tell.

The whites and the natives accepted each other and often crossed paths in town, in the woods, and on farms. Some Indians asked for food from the settlers, while others helped their new neighbors clearing land. The Miami and the Potawatomi tribes shared customs and events with their new neighbors.

In 1837, nearly a thousand Miami met at Seeks Village for a feast and dance. The Village had a regular population of about 150 to 200 people. Twenty to 30 encampment fires lighted the summer night sky, drawing in curious white neighbors from the area. Women prepared savory dishes of dog soup, venison, or bear steak. The settlers saw wild turkeys, feathers still intact, cooking on the fire.[23]

---

[22] Kaler, Samuel P., and Richard H. Maring. "History of Whitley County," Indiana. Indianapolis, Indiana: B.F. Bowen & Co., 1907, p. 123.
[23] Weston Arthur Goodspeed and Charles Blanchard, "Counties of Whitley and Noble, Historical and Biographical," Salem, Massachusetts: Higginson Book Co., 1992, p. 56.

Male warriors danced while fellow natives feasted with their white neighbors. Twenty Indians danced around a pole with a limping motion; another warrior, covered in an otter skin, yelled, "Poo-Poo" while encircling the pole. He stopped in front of a man, pointed, and yelled, "Poo-Poo" again. That individual fell to the ground, playing dead. The dance continued as others were tagged and played dead.

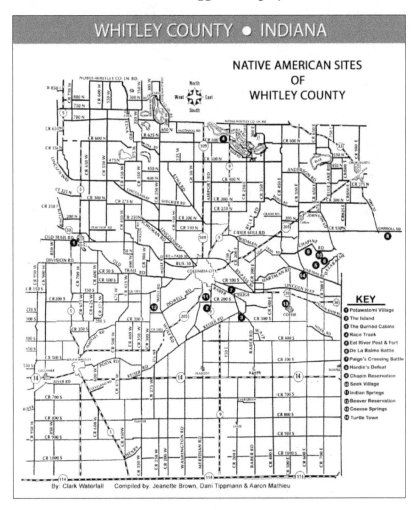

MAP OF WHITLEY COUNTY, NOTING LOCATIONS OF TRIBES AND ENCAMPMENTS. WHITLEY COUNTY HISTORICAL SOCIETY.

White men were generally curious about native customs, and especially healings and natural medicine. Rumors ran rampant through Whitley County, particularly about a rattlesnake bite cure. A Columbia City man described how an older woman cured an Indian boy. A young boy ran back into town from the woods. A rattlesnake had bitten the child, and the rattlesnake was still attached to the child's foot. An elderly native woman grabbed, defanged, and killed the snake. She ran a few yards into the nearby woods and came back, chewing on a mouthful of an herb the whites couldn't identify. She applied the now-prepared cud to the boy's foot. The herbs immediately drew out the poison. The indigenous people would not share their secrets with the whites about the healing herb's identification and properties.[24]

A popular activity witnessed by many settlers was the steam dance at Seeks Village. The Indians stacked dry wood with many stones on top. The pile was set on fire, the wood burned away, leaving the rocks scorching hot. The natives placed a large deer-skin wigwam over what remained of the fire, making the structure nearly airtight.[25]

Fifteen or 20 Indians and some settlers clad only in a breechclout—a buckskin piece tied at the waist with a thong between the legs—entered the wigwam. The participants threw water on the rocks, and the makeshift lodge filled with steam. For about half an hour, men danced around the fire, emerging with sweat pouring off. The next group added water to the hot stones and repeated the ritual of purification. Holistic healers of the modern era have adopted the steam dance ritual, believing it cleanses the body of chemicals and toxins.

In 1844, the federal government moved the Miami and the Potawatomi tribes to Kansas. Chief Coesse, whose Miami name was Pc-can-co-an-sah-Quah, accompanied the natives but returned to live out his life in Whitley County, where he died in 1854.[26] What has been lost from the customs and traditions of the natives is unknowable but undoubtedly significant. Many of their traditions, saved only in oral history, have vanished.[27]

---

[24] Weston Arthur Goodspeed and Charles Blanchard, "Counties of Whitley and Noble, Historical and Biographical," Salem, Massachusetts: Higginson Book Co., 1992, p. 56.

[25] Weston Arthur Goodspeed and Charles Blanchard, "Counties of Whitley and Noble, Historical and Biographical," Salem, Massachusetts: Higginson Book Co., 1992, p. 56.

[26] Historical Society Whitley County, Columbia City, Indiana, "1876 Illustrated Historical Atlas of Indiana," Accessed February 21, 2021. http://whitleycountyin.org/wc1876atlas.htm.

[27] Brown, Jeanette A. Index to Whitley County Biographies in the "Memorial Record of Northeastern Indiana," Chicago, the Lewis Publishing Company, 1896. Columbia City, IN: Genealogical Society of Whitley County, 2002.

The white man had come to Whitley County to stay. The indigenous peoples were relocated against their will from lands they had loved for centuries. Tree by tree, the unbroken forests would transform into farms and villages as far as the eye could see.

Amy McVay Abbott

9 Cultivating Community

Ohioans spread the word about Indiana's fertile soil and great opportunities, and growth exploded in Whitley County and northern Indiana. By 1838, four hundred and eleven 160-acre Whitley County farms had been sold by the Fort Wayne Land Patent Office. Growth brought government, new roads, and neighbors.

After a War of 1812 battle hero, Whitley County was named for Colonel William Whitley of Lincoln County, Kentucky. Townships were formally organized, and the nicknamed Swamp Township was named Washington Township, after our first President.

Reuben Long, a vocal Democrat, served as a township elector at Abraham Lesley's home in the 1840 presidential election. He joined 16 other male landowners, including Peter Creager's son Adam. Elizabeth and other wives stayed home. Women were nearly a century away from receiving the franchise. The 1840 election was the first presidential election in the new county.[28]

The Whig candidate Martin Van Buren won Whitley County by only seven votes. William Henry Harrison, who had served as Indiana's first territorial governor, and a Democrat, became president. Against prudent advice, Harrison gave a lengthy inaugural address on the U.S. Capitol steps in inclement weather. Harrison died of pneumonia only 31 days into the office on April 4, 1841.[29]

---

[28] Weston Arthur Goodspeed and Charles Blanchard, "Counties of Whitley and Noble, Historical and Biographical." Salem, Massachusetts: Higginson Book Co., 1992, page 202.
[29] Weston Arthur Goodspeed and Charles Blanchard, "Counties of Whitley and Noble, Historical and Biographical." Salem, Massachusetts: Higginson Book Co., 1992, page 202.

News of Harrison's victory arrived via *The* Detroit Free Press, one of the largest newspapers available in Whitley County, weeks after the election. Newspapers and letters were the primary sources of information in the 1840s. Information in Washington Township was procured in one of two ways. Families could wait for the South Whitley Postmaster to get the mail in Huntington or skip the middleman and go directly to Huntington to get the mail a few days early.

From the Washington [Pa.] Examiner—Extra.

DEATH OF THE PRESIDENT.

OFFICE OF THE GLOBE,
April 4, 2 o'clock, A. M.

It is with deep regret we announce that WILLIAM HENRY HARRISON IS NO MORE! He died at thirty minutes before one o'clock this morning. His disease was pleurisy, complicated with disordered liver and bowels, which from the first, bore a serious aspect.

All the efforts of the best medical skill and most unremitting attention were unavailable.

In announcing this melancholy event, all other reflections are absorbed in the thought of the nothingness of life, the emptiness of earthly grandeur. One brief month has witnessed his ascent to the summit of human ambition—and his passage to the tomb. "What shadows we are, and what shadows we pursue!"

Cleveland April 9th 5 o'clock P. M.

"DEATH OF THE PRESIDENT," DETROIT FREE PRESS, DETROIT, MICHIGAN, APRIL 12, 1841.

South Whitley was the nearest village for the rural settlers. While Columbia City later became the county seat, Cleveland Township and western Washington Township residents often went to the Eel River town for shopping and a trip to the mill.

The trip to South Whitley could be a bumpy ride on dirt roads with holes and surfaces affected by the weather. The Indiana Legislature, through the Three Percent Fund, upgraded county and state roads. Christian Creager helped build State Street, the unpaved main street in South Whitley, in 1838. State Street wasn't paved for another 80 years.[30]

In his late teens, Christian also helped build two miles of state roads in the summer of 1839. State roads were often made with timbers or planks, which then seemed a never-ending natural resource.

Reuben Long handled the problem of poor Washington Township roads with his ax. Reuben and other Washington Township men, Joseph Ecker, John Oliver, Jonas Baker, and Abraham Lesley, cut out new county roads in the early 1840s in the township along section lines. The men cut brush, stuffed the holes in the existing pathways, and then covered them with dirt. Gravel and rocks went on top. Reuben and the workers made the new roads as wide as a team of horses. Likely made

---

[30] "The Creager Family Heritage," Harriet F. Wright, 1958, Richmond, IN, reprinted and indexed by Florence Blanchard, 1979, Higuera, CA.

by this method were two primary roads in the township, Tunker Road and Washington Center Road.

The new roads crossed at the small village of Tunker, smack dab in the middle of Washington Township. The little town was named after its Dunkard settlers, a term from the old country. Both Dunkard and Tunker refer to the practice of submersion baptism or dunking.

The Longs and Creager men assisted in building the Tunker Church on the southwest corner of where the Tunker and Washington Center roads met. Many settlers who came from areas now called Germany were Catholic; many were Protestant, likely Lutheran. Reuben was raised in a community that embraced both Dunkard and Lutheran faith; Elizabeth Olinger's family was Dunkard. Peter Creager, Senior, and some of his older children were baptized in the Lutheran faith, but they spread out among various Protestant congregations after coming to Indiana. By the end of the 1840s, one could barely throw a rock in Whitley County without hitting a church building.

Most Protestant faiths were represented in Washington and Cleveland Townships, and Nix Settlement featured a sizeable Catholic parish with an itinerant priest.

Amy McVay Abbott

10 Expanding Families

Reuben sat outside his log home, next to the south-facing cabin door. waiting for his child's birth, Purple clematis vine threaded the fence around his house, winding up and over the split-rails Reuben and John built five years before. The cabin door was open, daring the sun to fill the room with light. Reuben could hear Elizabeth's wails. Her time was getting closer.

The couple treasured their son and daughters. Another child was about to arrive. Would this one be a boy? Pioneers with sons, like the Creagers, had a considerable advantage. Boys hunted and dressed their kill, cleared land, hauled timber, and assisted in planting and harvest. Women didn't usually help with heavy chores but kept the home fires burning. However, pioneer women had a certain toughness in unpredictable circumstances. Survival in a wild and unknown place took great emotional and physical fortitude, especially in bearing and raising children in the wilderness.

Reuben should have been working, but today he would wait for the baby's birth. Was he concerned? Childbirth was dangerous in the 19th century with little power over an infection and no anesthesia or pain control. Rural women did not see a doctor often, if ever. As had happened throughout time, a fair number of pioneer women and babies died in childbirth.

Whitley County had several traveling doctors who visited families in rural areas, but did not attend normal childbirth. Elizabeth's older daughter Catherine held her mother's hand and wiped her brow. A neighbor, also a mother, helped Elizabeth with the delivery. Elizabeth would reciprocate for her neighbors at their time.

One of Reuben's daughters told him a son had been born. Yes, it was a boy! Reuben was delighted. Reuben and Elizabeth named him "Lewis" after his grandfather, Reuben's father, who still lived in Ohio. Two more sons would follow for Reuben and Elizabeth, Washington Long in 1845, and Eliga Long in 1850.

∂

The fruits of Reuben and Elizabeth's labors enriched other aspects of their lives. Peach and Maiden Blush apple trees grew, planted in 1839, when rains didn't wash out everything planted as they had the prior year. Elizabeth and her children planted a vegetable and flower garden.

Money from the sale of timber meant more store-bought goods for the family. Reuben's oxen team considerably upped the farm's timber output. With additional funds, the Longs traveled to South Whitley more often on improved roads Reuben and others made.

A dry goods store opened in South Whitley near the Eel River. Elizabeth, driven by Reuben, could make the trip to South Whitley for coffee or tea, needles, thread, or larger items like a washboard or a broom. A pound of coffee cost about eighty cents.[31] The ready-made thread availability meant Elizabeth or her daughters didn't spend as much time at the spinning wheel. Most pioneer women put their wheels away in the mid-to-late 19th century. The constant whirr-whirr of the wheel was lost to memory.

Adam and Peter Creager, Junior, had moved to Washington Township from their father's home in Cleveland Township. Adam Creager was the first man to marry in Washington Township, wedding Susan Stoner in 1839. The other Creager children spread out throughout the county, owning good farmland, and carrying on their father's farming tradition.

On December 30, 1841, their brother Christian Creager married Susanna Obenchain, Samuel and Catharine Obenchain's daughter. Christian and Susanna were married in South Whitley and celebrated at her father's home.

While pioneer families did not have an extensive wardrobe, a wedding usually called for a new dress. Susanna Obenchain's parents purchased new fabric for her wedding dress. The wedding attire of the 1840s featured a lace collar, material appropriate to the season, and a full,

---

[31] "The History of What Things Cost in America: 1776 to Today." 247 Wall St. Accessed February 6, 2021. https://247wallst.com/investing/2010/09/16/the-history-of-what-things-cost-in-america-1776-to-today/2/.

ruffled petticoat underneath the long garment. Few brides wore impractical white in rural Indiana. Christian owned one suit and would wear it, as the saying goes, for marrying and burying.

Neighbors, old and young, came to the Obenchains' home to feast, dance, and celebrate the new marriage. Making as much noise as possible, Christian's brothers and friends belled the couple after supper—banging pans, shouting, shooting their guns to the sky. The uproar didn't stop until the bride and groom stepped outside, generally with food. Imagine the celebration with a December 30th wedding, almost New Year's Eve.

On the second evening, the belling was repeated, unmercifully, until Christian and Susanna appeared with more food. A second belling, a predictable event with two large families merging, raised a few South Whitley roofs, especially merry on New Year's Eve.[32]

Christian and Susanna lived in Cleveland Township, near both sets of parents. Christian Creager wanted a farm of his own but lacked the funds. He hired out to area farmers for more than 15 years, saving money for his farm. The young family boarded with Christian's employer or built a cabin on Samuel Obenchain's lots. Christian found other ways to bring in money, including shooting and trapping. He shot and skinned an otter, selling the hide for $8.50, about $300 in today's dollars.[33]

For Whitley County young people, reading, writing, and arithmetic were vital skills. The boys were encouraged to improve their figuring, so the timber or grain mills couldn't cheat them. Their future farms would be best served with educated owners. Girls, needed to help run the home, often dropped out of school around fourth grade. Many children learned to read from the Bible at home. While higher education was rare, most farmers in Whitley County—as census data indicated—could read and write by mid-century.

Children were also needed on the farm, so rural schools met only in the winter months. Reuben and Elizabeth and their neighbors paid a few

---

[32] The tradition of belling in Washington Township continued for a long time. The author's parents Marilyn Enz and Bill McVay were belled after their wedding in summer 1955.

[33] Kaler, Samuel P., and Richard H. Maring, "History of Whitley County, Indiana. Indianapolis, Indiana: B.F. Bowen & Co., 1907, p. 119.

dollars a year for their children's subscription school. Children started school after harvest and stopped school when it was time for planting.

In the early 1840s, Reuben helped build a log school in the middle of Section 8 in Washington Township. Reuben was the township trustee, so he called the shots for the school in his district. Many of the outlying neighbors weren't happy about the location, as the school had no central road access. The trustee defended his position, that the school was built in the best place for the pupils attending.

Perhaps Reuben held more sway because he was the trustee, and his father-in-law, Jacob Olinger, was the teacher. Among early students were the Long children, and students with familiar names, Weybright and Montz.

WASHINGTON TP.
b. 10 Aug. 1776 Frederick Co. Wash.
d. 16 Mch 1849 S. Whitley, Ind.

PETER CREAGER, SENIOR, DIED AT THE END OF THE 1840S, LEAVING A LARGE LEGACY IN WHITLEY COUNTY. FAMILY IMAGE.

Lighting the schoolhouse was a challenge as students attended during the darkest times of year. Early on, teachers used candles made from animal fat. The candles gave off a bright light but smelled awful. Using kerosene lamps with a wick, students could better see their lessons, and the odor was acceptable. Oil lamps, like candles before them, always posed a danger. Olinger kept an eye out for roughhousing, or an accidental upset of the lighting.[34]

The decade of the 1840s ended with Peter Creager's death in March. Peter, Senior, was the father of Christian and his siblings. Catharine Flora Obenchain, the mother of Susanna Creager, died a week later. Peter and Catharine were both buried in the Old Cleveland Township Cemetery at the western end of South Whitley.

---

34 McCord Museum. "Household Heating, Lighting and Hygiene in the 19th and 20th Centuries." Household Heating, Lighting and Hygiene in the 19th and 20th Centuries | Thematic Tours | Musée McCord Museum. McCord Museum. Accessed February 7, 2021.

23

I, Peter Creager of the County of Whitley in the State of Indiana, do make and publish this my last Will and Testament in manner and form following That is to say first it is my Will that my funeral expenses and all my just debts be fully paid. Second. I, give devise and bequeath to my beloved wife Elizabeth Creager the plantation on which we now reside situate lying and being a part of the North West quarter of Section Number thirteen (13) Township Number thirty (30) North Range Number Eight (8) East. Containing about one hundred and Twenty acres, during her natural life. And all the life Stock Horses Cattle Sheep, Hogs, &c by me now owned and Kept thereon. also all the household furniture and other Items not particularly named in this Will during her natural life as aforesaid she however first disposing of a sufficiency thereof to pay my just debts as aforesaid, and that at the death of my said wife, all the property hereby devised or bequeathed to her as aforesaid or so much thereof as may then remain unexpended, to my children, Sophia Creager, William Creager, Samuel Creager, Ezra Creager Adam Creager, Christian Henry Creager, Geo Creager Peter Creager, Lydia Margaret Creager, and John Reuben Creager and to their heirs and assigns forever in manner and form following, That is to say, share and share alike, provided however that my son Ezra Creager shall receive thirty dollars less because he has received one Horse heretofore worth thirty dollars, it is also my will that the children of my daughter Catharine Newman that is Eve Newman John Newman and Peter Newman each receive five dollars because my daughter Catharine having received the principal portion of her legacy heretofore And it is further my will that after the death of my wife Elizabeth Creager the property then remaining shall be sold and the proceeds thereof to be distributed in manner and form aforesaid and lastly, I hereby Constitute and appoint my said wife Eliza beth Creager and my son Adam Creager to be the Executors for this my last Will and Testament revoking and annuling all former Wills by me made and ratifying and confirming this and no other to be my last Will and Testament— In Testimony Whereof I have hereunto set my hand and seal this twelfth day of January in the year of our Lord one thousand eight hundred and forty nine—

Peter Creager {Seal}

WILL OF PETER CREAGER, SR., 1849.

55

Reuben and Elizabeth's daughter Catherine married Joseph Obenchain, son of Samuel and the late Catharine Flora Obenchain, on November 19, 1849. When he married, Joseph had a small tract of unimproved land in Cleveland Township, ultimately expanding to 540 acres. Joseph was, like his father and father-in-law, a Democrat. The family belonged to the Dunkard Church, and Joseph served as Township Trustee of Cleveland Township.

In 1848, Reuben's father, Lewis Long, died in Dayton, Ohio. His widow, Catherine Hiestand Long, moved to Whitley County for the rest of her life and lived with her son John in Washington Township.

By 1850, Whitley County boasted 941 dwellings, 522 farms, and eight manufacturing plants.[35] For those farm dwellers, the advent of the steel plow at mid-century meant easier planting for those who could afford it. While Whitley County was no longer the thinly-populated wilderness, farm life still faced brutal challenges from weather, disease, and surprises Mother Nature had in store.

---

[35] Kaler, Samuel P., and Richard H. Maring, "History of Whitley County, Indiana," Indianapolis, Indiana: B.F. Bowen & Co., 1907, p. 256.

11 What Hath God Wrought?

Jonas Baker continued to grow his farms, and also his poor reputation. *The Indiana Herald* published a weekly list of patrons who had not bothered to get their mail at the Post Office. Some in Washington Township, especially those on the southern end of the township, picked up their mail in Huntington. Jonas stayed on the shameful list for weeks at a time.

Mariah Haines Baker had given Jonas two daughters, Elizabeth and Ann Margaret, and a son, Daniel, in the few years after their 1843 marriage. How angry was Mariah when she waited on letters from her parents in Dayton? Or when she waited to mail a letter announcing a new baby? Handwritten notes were as precious to settlers as the gold Jonas carried in his pockets on his initial trip to Whitley County.

Because rural areas lagged in new technology, Jonas and Mariah didn't know the newly invented telegraph would change communication. In 1844, the year the Bakers' first child was born, Samuel Morse created a dot-dash code with alphabet letters and symbols. The Morse code, converted to electrical signals, traveled via a wire from one station to another. A telegraph operator tapped the dots and dashes with a metal piece on a wooden slab attached to the wire. Morse sent his first telegram, "What Hath God Wrought?" from Washington, D.C., to Baltimore.

But by 1852, when the Bakers' daughter Mary Jane arrived, the telegraph was available, while rural free mail delivery was still decades away. Settlers had a new way to communicate with relatives in Ohio and farther east. Franklin Pierce Baker, the Bakers' last child, was born a decade later. For rural people, sending a telegraph involved a trip to Columbia City. Still, it allowed their distant family to receive important news in a day, such as the announcement of Franklin Pierce Baker's birth.

The Long family was also growing larger. Two older Long children married. Jacob married Mary Fox in 1855, and Sarah Long married Lewis Weybright in 1856. Reuben became more dependent on his younger sons, who still lived at home. Young Lewis, Washington, and Eliga all had farm chores. Reuben's son Lewis was becoming a man, and he needed his assistance for the most challenging work on the Indiana farm.

The county seat, Columbia City, grew with added commerce and population after the opening of the Fort Wayne and Chicago Railroad in 1856.[36] A patron could leave Columbia City at 7:00 a.m. and arrive in Fort Wayne with breathtaking speed by 9:30 a.m. Leaving Fort Wayne at 5 p.m., one could arrive home even more quickly by 6:30 p.m. The trip by horse and wagon took far longer and generally required an overnight stay.

In the quarter of a century since Reuben and other pioneers came to northeastern Indiana, daily life challenges were not nearly as complex. Shortly, that would all change with personal, horrific consequences for many Whitley County families. There was a fissure in the country, a volcanic crack between north and south that reached Indiana and the farm on Sugar Creek. A War Between the States was brewing, and the pot soon boiled over in South Carolina.

---

[36] "1876 Illustrated Historical Atlas of Indiana," Historical Society Whitley County, Columbia City Indiana Genealogical, Accessed February 5, 2021. http://whitleycountyin.org/wc1876atlas.htm. "Whitley County Atlas."

12 Reporting for Duty

The drumbeat of civil war pounded louder each day. Whitley County residents argued about the whys and wherefores, and everyone agreed war with the South was inevitable. Some settlers wanted the Union preserved without slavery. Most Hoosiers disliked slavery and hated the idea of war, and many settlers had moved away from southern slave-holding states. Some believed that the South should become a sovereign country. And many young men were eager to enlist, despite protestations of worried mothers.

One by one, southern states seceded, and the Union refused to recognize the new Confederacy. The attack on Fort Sumpter at Charleston, South Carolina, started the war in April 1861, shortly after President Abraham Lincoln's first inauguration.

The unexpected death of Reuben Long on June 19, 1861 pre-empted much of the war talk in the Long family. For Elizabeth, the war was secondary to her husband's untimely passing.

Reuben, who died without a will, was buried near the sanctuary at Eberhard Lutheran Church. Reuben and most of his family worshipped at Brethren (sometimes called Dunkard or Mennonite) churches in Whitley County. His Prussian ancestors were Lutheran, and while living in Virginia, his family embraced the doctrines of the pacifist Brethren.

With Reuben's demise, the weight of the world fell on 58-year-old Elizabeth's shoulders with three sons left at home. Elizabeth's three older children, Jacob, Catherine, and Sarah were all married. Jacob Long and wife Mary, and Sarah and husband Lewis Weybright lived on neighboring farms, while Catherine and husband Joseph Obenchain lived in Cleveland Township, a few miles west. All three couples were busy raising their families.

Eighteen-year-old Lewis Reuben, 15-year-old Washington, and 11-year-old Eliga stepped up their work on the farm with their father gone. Lewis and Washington were ready for the increased challenges; their father had taught them well. Eliga had many chores, but he was only 11 and couldn't do a man's job. The farm needed all hands on deck with Reuben gone.

The Long brothers imagined themselves in official blue uniforms, defending the Union, and spent hours imagining the war, despite their mother's protestations and grief.

Elizabeth couldn't stop her sons from continually talking about it, although as a Dunkard, she couldn't condone war. Cousins and friends from Whitley County volunteered for the Union Army in droves. What didn't help her case was that her late husband had often bragged about the bravery of his grandfather, Henry Long, who served in the Fifth Virginia Regiment of the Revolutionary War. Henry had volunteered in his sixties, long past the age where he could provide much physical support. By the end of the Revolutionary War, the colonists were seeking recruits of all ages.

Elizabeth protested her son's war talk. Not every young man had a newly widowed mother at home and acreage in need of year-round care.

Reuben and Elizabeth had been married for nearly 37 years. He was 60 when he passed; she was two years younger. Despite initial trials in their first years in the Hoosier wilderness, Reuben and Elizabeth built a successful farm and life together. Reuben left the family in decent circumstances, with the 1860 census valuing his owned property at $3,000 and more than $500 in personal assets.[37]

Elizabeth held close what she and Reuben built. What would happen to the farm was not clear to her or any of the children. So Lewis, Washington, and Eliga kept the farm going under their mother's direction. The farm ownership would not be resolved for more than a decade until well after Reuben's widow passed.

Elizabeth mulled over her family situation. Eliga was still her baby, her youngest child, barely old enough to use his rifle. Washington, already a firebrand, was only 15 but talked about enlisting. Would he lie about his age and enlist, as others did? Lewis, the couple's second-oldest son after Jacob, was already 18. He was old enough to join the military, and most

---

[37] U.S. Census Bureau. Federal Census 1860, Washington Township, Whitley County, Indiana, Roll M653_307, page 907, Family History Library film 803307, Provo, Utah, accessed February 23, 2021.

of his friends had enlisted. His mother couldn't stop him. It was a matter of time before he followed the other young men.

News poured in from far-away battlefields with unfamiliar names like Shiloh and Bull Run. Citizens argued in the opinion pages of local newspapers, public spaces, and over their supper tables.

Six thousand people attended the Fourth of July events in Columbia City. The Long boys watched the parade of uniformed volunteers in the Whitley Calvary and Whitley Artillery. At the fairgrounds, a program opened with prayer followed by a reading of the Declaration of Independence. A children's choir sang "Independence Day," and after more speeches, the day ended with a large picnic.[38]

Political fervor rose with talk of a federal draft. Young men practiced shooting, while women knitted scarves and socks for the soldiers headed into battle. Tunker and South Whitley, and every Whitley County village, had offices for signing recruits. Still no draft but more men were needed on the western front, along the Mississippi River.

> On July 9, 1862, a local paper reported that "The Government calls for three hundred thousand volunteers. The number must be raised, even if drafting shall become necessary. The West has already done her share by furnishing men for this war and with no doubt be ready to furnish all that may be asked of her."[39]

Lewis was conflicted. If he enlisted, the work would fall on his brother Washington. But Washington was tough as nails and would handle about anything life threw him.

Lewis told his heartbroken mother that summer he was going to enlist. He joined on August 11, 1862. The young men of Whitley County responded to the government's call. Lewis traveled to Fort Wayne along with many other Whitley County volunteers. He was now Private Lewis Long, Indiana 88th Infantry, Company K.

❧

---

[38] Weston Arthur Goodspeed and Charles Blanchard, "Counties of Whitley and Noble, Indiana, Historical and Biographical" Salem, MA: Higginson Book Co., 1992, p.106.
[39] "The New Call." The Indiana Herald. Huntington, Indiana, July 9, 1862.

Serving in the Union Army, Lewis quickly learned, was no Fourth of July picnic. Instead of the bounty of food Elizabeth served the family morning, noon, and night, Lewis received a daily ration of meat and bread. The government had a salt pork plant in Chicago, so soldiers in the western Army often had salt pork or bacon on their menu. The Army didn't provide any fresh fruits or vegetables or dairy. Still, a savvy quartermaster could convince patriotic farmers to donate eggs or milk or fruits or vegetables.

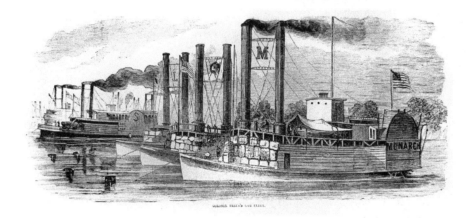

MISSISSIPPI MARINE BRIGADE RAM SHIP. IMAGE IN PUBLIC DOMAIN.

Private Long fought in one of the deadliest battles of the war, the Battle of Stones River in Kentucky and Tennessee. Twenty-six thousand men—both Union and Confederate soldiers—died in the bluegrass. Long survived.

With his Company still camped near Murfreesboro, in the spring of 1863, Lewis mustered out and transferred to the Mississippi Marine Brigade on March 30 at St. Louis.[40] The Mississippi Marine Brigade (MMB) had long interested Lewis because of its reputation for intrigue and spies. The MMB may have been the Navy Seals of its day. About 350 soldiers staffed the MMB unit, patrolling and protecting the Mississippi River. With battle and espionage duties, the MMB worked behind the scenes and other times in direct battle. With a fleet of nine light-armored boats, the MMB was renowned for sneaking and ramming the sides of a Confederate ship, causing the boat to sink.

---

[40] "https://Secure.in.gov/Apps/Iara/Search/Home/Detail?RId=1210249." Indiana Archives and Records Administration. State of Indiana government. Accessed February 23, 2021.

Under Lt. Col. George E. Currier, Lewis and his fellow soldiers protected the Union shore and thwarted Confederate attacks on Union ships and land.[41] The soldiers worked quickly over four days to build a fort across from Vicksburg, Mississippi. Railroad iron covered the fort's walls, which were outfitted with a Parrott gun facing east across the river to Vicksburg. Union soldiers fired 98 rounds from the 1800-pound iron Parrott gun throughout June 23 and gained the Confederates' attention on the other side of the river. The weapon found its target, damaging the Confederate foundry and machine shop. Confederates returned fire, hitting but not severely damaging the fort. All the Union soldiers, including Lewis, survived.[42] The Union ultimately won at Vicksburg. Vicksburg may have been given short shrift in the history books, with the bloody 3-day Battle of Gettysburg happening simultaneously in Pennsylvania.

Late in the summer of 1863, Lewis became ill with dysentery. Poor sanitation and contaminated water sent dysentery throughout both the Union and Confederate armies. Army hospitals, on both sides of the Mississippi River overflowed with ill soldiers. Diseases swept through the hospitals because of contaminated water, vermin, and filthy conditions. Having few supplies, medical personnel used linens and towels on multiple patients, spreading dysentery, cholera, and other diseases to those in the hospitals.

Lewis's health worsened, and he died of dysentery in a military hospital in Cairo, Illinois, on September 10, 1863, 400 miles from home. He was buried at what later became a national cemetery at Mound City, Illinois. While the War Department notified his mother in Whitley County, no family member could visit his burial site during an active war time.

---

[41] "U.S.S. Autocrat, flagship of the Marine Brigade, Mississippi River, May-July 1863, artist's impression, zoomable image," House Divided: The Civil War Research Engine at Dickinson College, http://hd.housedivided.dickinson.edu/node/40688.

[42] "United States Mississippi Marine Brigade." National Parks Service. U.S. Department of the Interior. Accessed February 23, 2021. https://www.nps.gov/vick/learn/historyculture/united-states-mississippi-marine-brigade.htm.

GRAVE OF PRIVATE LEWIS REUBEN LONG,
MOUND CITY, ILLINOIS.
IMAGE PROVIDED BY WINFIELD MAINE.

The Long family kept the home fires burning for nearly two more years for the war's duration. At full adulthood, Washington was only about five foot seven inches tall but powerfully built and muscular after years of hard work on the farm. He was good with people and shrewd in business and gradually fell into the farm's management role.

13 Intestate

Nearly 25 years had passed since Reuben first set foot in Indiana. While the farm remained unchanged, the family did not. When Reuben, the family patriarch, died without a will in June 1861, the estate reverted to Elizabeth. She managed with her sons' assistance until Lewis enlisted in the Union Army. According to the title deed for the property, Elizabeth's inheritance taxes were $3.20 on a valuation of $3,000 in personal property and $4,000 in real estate. This represented an unexplained increase from the 1860 census data which showed less personal property and real estate.[43]

Lewis Long's death in the Civil War brought tremendous grief to the family.

Washington and Eliga held up as best they could; Washington had an aptitude for agriculture and soon made money for the farm. Yet, Washington did not own the farm and couldn't make any changes or improvements without his mother or siblings' blessing.

Over the next decade, Washington grew in his love and talent for growing things. Elizabeth died in February 1870, and buried at Eberhard Cemetery. Washington's grandmother, Catherine Hiestand Long, died in August and was also buried at Eberhard. She was 97 and had lived with Reuben's brother John and his family since she came from Ohio after her husband's death in 1848.

The following year Washington married the daughter of neighbors Jonas and Mariah Baker. Mary Jane Baker used her middle name, Jane. She had

---

[43] In the Matter of the Estate of Reuben Long (Legal Document Probate Order Book A page 440, Whitley County, Indiana, Court of Pleas, October 22, 1861.

been a playmate of Washington's since they were children in district schools.

Eliga moved out when Washington and Jane married. He moved in with his sister Sarah and her husband Lewis Weybright. At the time of Washington's marriage, his parents' estate was not yet settled. Washington still did not own the farm, so he and Jane lived in the second log cabin that Reuben built in 1836, unable to build their own home on property they did not own.

The older children and spouses of Reuben and Elizabeth Long, Jacob and Mary Long, Sarah and Lewis Weybright, and Catherine and Joseph Obenchain, relinquished their shares in the farm to Washington and Eliga via quit claim in 1871.

```
Joseph Obenchain and          )  Warranty Deed.
Catharine Obenchain, his      )  Dated, December 15, 1871.
wife, Lewis Weybright and     )  Recorded, December 18, 1871.
Sarah Weybright, his wife,    )  Recorded in Deed Record "X"
Jacob Long and Mary M. Long,  )  page 127.
His wife,                     )  Consideration, $2600.00.
          to                  )
Washington Long and Elijah    )
     Long.

          The parties of the first part of Whitley County,

Indiana, convey and warrant to the second parties of the same

place, the following real estate in Whitley County, Indiana,

to-wit:

          The Northeast quarter (¼) of Section No. Eighteen

(18), in Township No. Thirty (30) North, Range Nine East,

containing one hundred and sixty acres, more or less.

          "Signed"            Joseph Obenchain      (Seal)
                              Catharine Obenchain   (Seal)
                              Lewis Weybright       (Seal)
Witness                       Sarah Weybright       (Seal)
C. B. Tulley.                 Jacob E. Long         (Seal)
                                       her
                              Mary M.   x  Long     (Seal)
                                       mark

          Acknowledged by Joseph Obenchain, Catharine Obenchain,

Lewis Weybright, Sarah Weybright, Jacob Long and Mary M. Long,

December 18, 1871, before Eli W. Brown, Clerk, Whitley Circuit

Court, Whitley County, Indiana. (Seal).
```

It was a remarkable gift—Washington and Eliga held the farm together during the dozen years since their father died, including caring for their widowed mother. By law, the siblings could have divided the farm but valued their brothers' sweat equity.

After being married a year, Washington and Jane had their first child, a girl named Ida. Tragically, Ida became sick and died at the age of six months and 19 days. Ida was also buried at Eberhard Cemetery. Jane gave birth to their second child, Willie, on June 7, 1873, and he died the same day. The State of Indiana did not require death certificates for another decade, so there is no record of either cause of death.

The world was in another cholera epidemic that hit hard in Indiana in 1873.[44]   Indiana had cholera epidemics on and off since 1832, and citizens argued over the cause. Science now knows that water used for both drinking and sewage exacerbated the contagion.

> "The main form of treatment for cholera, as advised by the New York Health Department in 1873, was simply to constantly disinfect everything that came into contact with a person infected with cholera. Water closets, drains, seats, floors, containers holding discharges, clothing, sheets, towels, etc., were all to be disinfected and aired out. Damp cellars were advised to have fresh stone lime inside to absorb moisture; doors were kept open to promote airflow. Good health required one to drink pure water, be exposed to fresh air, eat substantial food, rest often, and bathe frequently."[45]

Without electricity and modern conveniences, keeping cholera out of homes was nearly impossible. Eliga died at age 23, likely from cholera, at his sister's home five months after his nephew was born and died.[46] Washington was Eliga's heir, one of eight siblings to own the legacy farm outright and change the future for his descendants.

Washington loved the farm that surrounded bubbling Sugar Creek. He cared for prized rich fields, the woods of walnut trees, the banks of wild-flowers along the creek, and the symmetry of cornrows he planted so carefully. After gaining full ownership of the farm, he built a new home for his family, and began expanding his livestock.[47]

---

[44] Rubrake, Natasha. "1873: Cholera Infects the Midwest," *Indiana Disasters Blog*, May 2014. https://indianadisasters.blogspot.com/2014/05/1873-cholera-infects-midwest.html.

[45] Rubrake, Natasha. "1873: Cholera Infects the Midwest," *Indiana Disasters Blog*, May 2014. https://indianadisasters.blogspot.com/2014/05/1873-cholera-infects-midwest.html.

[46] "Note from the *Indianapolis Journal*," *The Indiana Herald*, Huntington, Indiana, August 20, 1873.

[47] Kaler, Samuel P., and Richard H. Maring, "History of Whitley County, Indiana" Indianapolis, Indiana: B.F. Bowen & Co., 1907, p. 544.

14 Curiosity

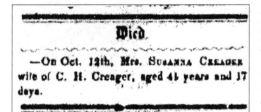

By 1860, Christian Henry Creager had relocated his family to Richland Township, north of South Whitley. Christian served the first of two terms as County Commissioner for Whitley County when his wife, Susanna, died in 1862 from typhoid fever. Christian was lonely and traveled back to Ohio to marry a woman he knew in his youth, Elizabeth Banfill Mettert, a widow with three children. The couple had four more children, Joseph, Oscar, Melissa, and Laura.

Christian Henry Creager

IMAGES PROVIDED BY MICHAEL ALEXANDER.

Christian Henry Creager came to Whitley County with his parents in 1836. He left 12 children to carry on his legacy of civic engagement.

Christian lived in several areas of the country, and his South Whitley home was a center of family life.

Catherine Creager, known as Kate, was Christian's second child by his first wife. Even though her mother died when Kate was 17, she was always surrounded by siblings, aunts and uncles, and many cousins. The Creagers were a close bunch who gathered often in family groups.

John Tyler Hoard's early life had not been so fortunate, having lived on his own since early childhood. John had been abandoned at age five by his father, Kellis Hord (sic), in Coshocton, Ohio. When John's mother, Angelina Moore Hord, died of scarlet fever, as did several of his siblings in 1845, Kellis deserted the family, including son John.

According to family oral tradition, Kellis Hord was a physician who was distraught about his inability to prevent his family members' deaths. He owned a nursery at one time in Coshocton, and city directories place him in the Cleveland area later, but there is no record of his death or burial.

John lived in an orphanage during early childhood. At 12, he went to Columbus, Ohio, to work as an errand boy in the Cadwalader Hotel on High Street. After two years, he accepted a position as a rope maker in a factory in Galena, 20 miles north of Columbus, where he stayed until he enlisted in the Union Army on May 17, 1861.[48]

John, whose Army records noted he had black hair and green eyes, saw much action in the infantry. He served until he developed dysentery and

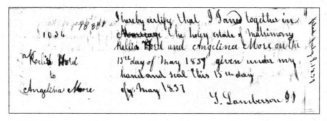

1839 WEDDING NOTICE FOR KELLIS HORD AND ANGELINA MOORE, COSHOCTON, OHIO. ANCESTRY.COM FILES: OHIO, USA, COUNTY MARRIAGES, 1774-1993.

was discharged a few months after enlisting. As soon as he was well, he re-upped in the Ohio Volunteers, where he served in the infantry

---

[48] "John T. Hoard Has Passed Through Many Scenes and Phases of Life," *The Commercial*, Columbia City, Indiana, April 22, 1896.

through the war's end. John fought under Union General George McClellan at Romney and Rich Mountain. He also saw action at Cross Keys, the Second Battle of Bull Run, and Gettysburg. "Gettysburg was the turning point of the war," he recalled.[49]

JOHN TYLER HOARD. FAMILY PHOTO.

When he was discharged honorably from the Union Army, John walked west through Ohio and stopped in Whitley County, Indiana, near the village of Lorane. John landed in Richland Township, which he found a "curiosity." There, in 1865, he met and married Kate Creager.[50]

Kate bore seven children at home in their log cabin: Peter, Alice, LeNore, Myrta, Henry Kellis, Archie, and Charles. A few years before Kate's passing and while she was ill, John and Kate lived in Lorane north of the Lorane store. Kate's 1885 death exacerbated John's trauma and shell shock from the Civil War battles he witnessed. He developed an addiction to alcohol.

---

[49] "John T. Hoard Has Passed Through Many Scenes and Phases of Life," *The Commercial,* Columbia City, Indiana, April 22, 1896.

[50] "John T. Hoard Has Passed Through Many Scenes and Phases of Life," *The Commercial,* Columbia City, Indiana, April 22, 1896.

While the Hoard siblings supported each other, their father was in and out of the picture, often for rehab at Veterans' hospitals in Marion and West Lafayette. With John no longer able to support the children, they were separated and sent to live with relatives or friends. Remarkably, they stayed close for the rest of their lives.

1865 WEDDING NOTICE FOR JOHN TYLER HOARD AND CATHERINE CREAGER, WHITLEY COUNTY, INDIANA. ANCESTRY.COM FILES: INDIANA, USA, MARRIAGES, 1810-2001.

CATHERINE "KATE" CREAGER.
IMAGE COURTESY OF MICHAEL ALEXANDER.

JOHN T. HOARD.

Has Passed Through Many Changing Scenes and Phases of Life.

We have in our city many historic personages and among the many we find one who has seen the dark side of life for 56 years—John T. Hoard.

Mr. Hoard was born March 4, 1840, in Coshocton, Ohio, and was left an orphan at the age of five years. When he reached the age of 12 he went to Columbus, Ohio, and was engaged as errand boy at the Cadwalader hotel on East High street. He worked over two years at that place and then accepted a position with a rope maker twenty miles north of Columbus in Delaware county, near the village of Galena and remained there until the outbreak of the late war. He was one of the first to enlist on the 17th day of May, 1861, at the city of Delaware, Delaware county, and served three months in the 4th Ohio Infantry. He re-enlisted in 1862 in the Ohio Volunteers.

While in the first service he was engaged in the battles of Romney and Rich Mountain under McClellan.

During the last three years' service he was engaged in the battle of Cross Keys, second battle of Bull Run and the memorable battle of Gettysburg which he thinks was the turning point of the war.

At the close of the war he passed over the northern states curiosity seeking and came to Whitley county in 1867. He has perhaps worked at more different kinds of work than any other man in the county. He can do anything pertaining to the farm such as stacking grain, shearing sheep, milking cows and churning, and can swing the axe and draw the cross-cut saw as well as the average woodman. John has helped to make the brick in the court house, west end school building, Clugston and Rhodes' blocks. We understand that he is a champion corn husker.

He is certainly a self-made man having acquired the larger part of his education outside of school hours, burning midnight oil for he is generally informed far above the average in history and scripture and always makes his point in argument. He is a Universalist in faith but does not claim to practice christianity.

Had he left intoxicants alone and made use of his natural ability he might have been numbered among the leading men of our country. We now find him employed at the Chambers House where he goes by the title of handy man. While he is 56 years old he would no doubt pass readily, should he go where he is not known, for a man of 35. He is very active for a man of his age.

COLUMBIA CITY COMMERCIAL, APRIL 22, 1896.

15 Expansion

In the 1870s, farmers consisted half the population of the United States. With 18 million of 38 million people farming, the average size per farm was 153 acres.[51] A farmer could feed his family and make a living on a farm that size, and the Long brothers did well on their farms in Washington Township.

Despite their losses, the latter part of the 1870s brought three healthy children to the Washington and Jane Long family. A son, Franklin, arrived in 1874,

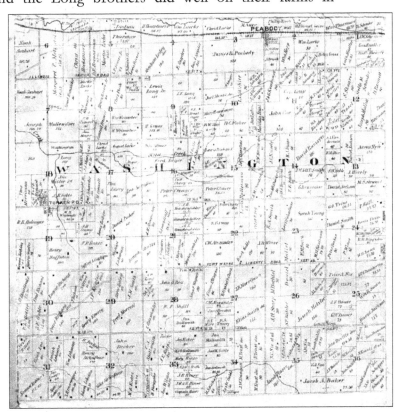

MAP OF WASHINGTON TOWNSHIP 1883. IMAGE FROM PUBLIC DOMAIN.

---

[51] Bellis, Mary. "Detailed Timelines of the History of American Agriculture." ThoughtCo. Accessed February 6, 2021. https://www.thoughtco.com/history-of-american-agriculture-farm-machinery-4074385.

Huntington Plow

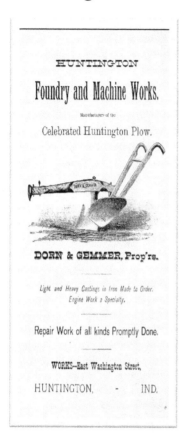

John Deere invented the iron plow around 1845. A foundry in neighboring Huntington, Indiana, released a version called the Huntington plow. An iron plow could cut through clods of soil far easier than a wooden one, easing the burden of the pioneers in Whitley County. Image source: The Indiana Herald, September 16, 1886.

followed by another son, Calvin, in 1875. Anna, their daughter, arrived in 1877.

While Washington continued to have many challenges in life, the business of farming was successful for him. The reaper-binder invented by Charles Baxter Withington in 1872 came into active use in Whitley County in the late 1870s. An improvement over McCormick's reaper, this machine allowed farms to cut the small-grain crop and also bind the stems into bundles or sheaves. Grain was shocked into cones that resembled tiny teepees and left to dry before being threshed. Teams of horses pulled the binders of this era; decades later, the horses were replaced by tractors, and ultimately, the modern combine.

What was initially called the Great Depression in 1873 was renamed the Panic of 1873 when the 1930s financial troubles came. Farmers had always been self-sufficient and rarely got involved in the stock market. Most families coped with inflation and the shortages of goods. The Panic started in Europe with the crash of their stock market and ultimately came to the United States when Europeans who had money in American railroads quickly sold their stocks. Indiana had experienced great prosperity and expansion after the Civil War and was less affected by the Panic than other parts of the country.[52]

The state of Indiana gave Washington and other farmers some help in 1875 with legislation mandating all County Commissioners must hear and address petitions for the location of ditches. In the old Swamp Township, water flow in and out of a man's acreage was still crucial to a crop's success. By 1881, the state curtailed part of

---

[52] Anderson, Jon. "The Panic of 1873." History of Indiana. Accessed February 1, 2021. http://thisisindiana.angelfire.com/history.htm.

the County Commissioners' power, transferring it to the Circuit Court. The state had, however, set in motion the superior management of ditches for the broader community.[53]

Washington gained in reputation as a local farmer and community activist. A local historian wrote this contemporary account of Washington.

> Prominent among the successful farmers and stock raisers of Whitley County is Washington Long. He has well improved his land with excellent buildings, good fences, and ample drainage, being one of the most pleasing and most productive farmers, not only in Washington township but in the county of Whitley as well.
>
> In addition to agriculture, Mr. Long is extensively engaged in the raising of livestock, feeding nearly all the products of the farm to his cattle and hogs, which he disposes of in large numbers. He makes a specialty of Shorthorn cattle and Chester White hogs of which he has earned a wide reputation, and his efforts in the matter of fine stock have induced many of his neighbors to imitate his example and improve their breeds of domestic animals.[54]

Washington's world was turned upside down when his wife Jane died in 1880, leaving him with three small children. In 1881 Washington lost his Uncle John Long, his father Reuben's beloved brother. John Long had passed away on the farm he staked in 1835, having been a successful farmer and civic-minded individual.

In 1882, Washington traveled to Van Wert County, Ohio, and married Albina Adelaide Flagg, the widow of Franklin Heath. She had no children, and Washington's children accepted her quickly as their mother. Albina was friendly and fashionable, and brought new life into the home of Washington Long.

---

[53] Goodspeed, Weston Arthur, and Charles Blanchard, "Counties of Whitley and Noble, Indiana: Historical and Biographical," Illustrated. Tucson, Ariz: Filmed by W.C. Cox Co., 1974, p. 16.
[54] Kaler, Samuel P., and Richard H. Maring, "History of Whitley County, Indiana," Indianapolis, Indiana: B.F. Bowen & Co., 19-07, pp. 543-544.

1893 LONG FAMILY PORTRAIT. WASHINGTON AND ALBINA, SEATED. STANDING (LEFT TO RIGHT), ANNA, FRANKLIN, CALVIN. FAMILY PHOTO.

16 The Fourth Richest Man in Washington Township

"He arose from the table, saying 'I will settle this,' and picking up his revolver, a 32-caliber British bulldog pattern, stepped to the porch and in the presence of his family and son-in-law David Shoemaker, placed the revolver to his right temple and fired, the bullet penetrating his brain. He lingered until 9:39 a.m. when he died. The result is what has been expected, as he often threatened to perform such an act."[55]

No one was the least bit surprised when Jonas Baker shot himself in the temple, in full view of his wife, his adult daughter, and her husband.

The word of his death spread quickly from farm to farm. Even his grand-children Anna, Franklin, and Calvin Long—children of his late daughter Mary Jane—weren't that surprised. Grandpa Baker had quite the reputation and not in a good way. The Long children's visits with their maternal grandfather were limited by Washington and Albina, believing reduced contact in their children's best interest.

But the Tunker area was a small place, and the children ran into their grandfather frequently. They enjoyed seeing their aunts and uncles, particularly Joseph and Elizabeth Baker Mullendore and their children. The Mullendore farm was north of Washington Long's farm.

Jonas had been a local legend since he arrived in the 1830s, barefoot, an ax over his shoulder. At only 18, Jonas came to Whitley County with

---

[55] "Through the Brain: Well-Known Farmer of Whitley County Kills Himself in the Presence of His Family." *The Democrat*, Huntington, Indiana, July 17, 1890.

enough gold coins to buy 320 acres of Washington Township land within his first years. That amount was double the typical purchase of 160 acres.

At his prime, Jonas owned one of the largest and most productive parcels in the township. Yet, in his sixties, Jonas still was the source of much gossip. As his grandson, J.A. Mullendore, recalled, "He was a character. Kind to some and generous to others who praised him highly."[56]

That praise, however, was not the whole story of the man.[57] Jonas frequently took his team of fine horses to a nearby town and visited a tavern. He stabled his team and wagon at the best livery stable and enjoyed a bender for a week or two. Jonas frequented public houses in Columbia City or Huntington, where he drank to excess.

Jonas was happy to spend money on his horses, but for himself, not so much. Rather than book a hotel, Jonas might drop in on a friend or someone he barely knew, entering their home late at night without their knowledge or permission. He announced himself to the surprised and sometimes fearful family in the morning.

Jonas didn't like the latest styles. So disgusted was he by women wearing silk that he often walked behind them and wet the backs of their dresses. Records don't reveal the source of the liquid; regardless, Jonas left his mark.

He was a physically large, tough, and a rough man with an unpredictable temper, and most people were afraid of him. Lewis Weybright, a neighbor, and son-in-law of Washington Long, drove Baker's team home from Columbia City while Jonas was asleep in the wagon box. When Lew crossed the rough swinging bridge over Sugar Creek, the team, the wagon, and the men were thrown into the water. Jonas blamed Lew and grabbed him by the neck and beat him with a brush.

Another time, lightning struck one of Baker's cattle during a storm, and Jonas shook his fist at the sky and defied God to burn him. After the storm, Jonas took the steer and the family Bible to his woods. He burned the steer and the Bible on the same fire.

---

[56] *Words of J.A. Mullendore*, e-mail from Susan Abentrod, Birmingham, Michigan, August 10, 2006. Also noted on Jonas Baker's gallery page in Ancestry.com.
[57] *Words of J.A. Mullendore*, e-mail from Susan Abentrod, Birmingham, Michigan, August 10, 2006. Also noted on Jonas Baker's gallery page in Ancestry.com.

Jonas was originally from Stark County, Ohio. After spending a few years in Whitley County, he returned to Ohio to marry Mariah Haines. Her family was originally from Pennsylvania but had moved west to Montgomery County. Jonas and Mariah had five children, including Mary Jane, known as Jane, who would become Washington Long's wife and the maternal grandfather to Franklin, Calvin, and Anna Long. Jonas and Mariah Baker also had four other children, Elizabeth, Ann Margaret, Daniel, and Franklin Pierce.

Yet, as Jonas's grandson also recalled, "He was known to ride horseback to the home of a poor settler, not aiming to be seen, and leaving a sack of cornmeal and a sack of potatoes."[58]

At the height of his farming career, Jonas had real estate valued at $12,800 and personal possessions valued at $1,950, making him the fourth richest man in the township after fellow farmers Noah Swihart, Jacob Metz, and Frederick Morrell. He kept beautiful horses, grew productive crops, and served several terms as a trustee of Washington township.[59]

In 1887, Mariah Baker died and two years later Jonas suffered another loss when his daughter Jane Long died. While his fortunes continued to grow, so did Baker's drinking and carousing. Within several years, Jonas was looking for a second wife. *The Huntington Democrat* printed a blurb in early June 1890.

> According to *The South Whitley News*, it cost Jonas Baker $2,000 for his bride, Mrs. Emma Lee, the Lee Hotel's proprietress in South Whitley. Mrs. Lee acted on the theory that a business should have the preference when business and pleasure meet.
>
> The dashing groom was informed that the root of all evil had very much to do with his success as a woo'er (sic), and it would be necessary for him to produce a sufficient amount to induce her to love forever, cherish and obey his lordship.
>
> But nothing daunted the prospective bridegroom, and his wallet was soon forthcoming, and the sum of about $2,000 was the price of his victory in the conquest.[60]

---

[58] *Words of J.A. Mullendore*, from Susan Abentrod, Birmingham, Michigan, August 10, 2006 to author. Also noted on Jonas Baker's gallery page in Ancestry.com.
[59] "Jonas Baker (1822-1890) - Find A Grave Memorial." Find a Grave. Accessed February 24, 2021. https://www.findagrave.com/memorial/26846732/jonas-baker.
[60] "South Whitley News." *The Democrat*, Huntington, Indiana, June 9, 1890.

In the end, Jonas handed over a bundle to Emma Lee, who, as a hotel owner, knew her way around a balance sheet. Mrs. Lee married Jonas Baker on June 5, 1890, and he promised, along with the sizeable wad of cash given, that he would not drink anymore. Can an old horse learn new tricks?

On July 14, barely a month after they were married, Jonas went to Huntington. He returned home violently drunk and insisted that all his family—his wife, daughter, and her husband—vacate the house. Then he went to the barn to sleep it off. The next morning Jonas came to the house for breakfast, and the new Mrs. Baker asked to have a word with him. She told him she was moving back to South Whitley as he had broken his promise to stop drinking.

Jonas rose from the table and took his gun, a 32-caliber British bulldog revolver. He stepped from the kitchen to the porch and shouted, "I will settle this." Then he shot himself in the right temple, in full view of the new Mrs. Baker, his daughter Ann Margaret, and son-in-law David Shoemaker.

The bullet penetrated his brain. Some reports note that he shot himself twice in the temple or that another person may have fired another shot. Jonas lingered for a few hours until he passed. No

THROUGH THE BRAIN.

A Well-Known Farmer of Whitley County Kills Himself in the Presence of His Family.

Jonas Baker, a well-to-do farmer living about six miles southeast of South Whitley, shot himself early Tuesday morning. He had been to this city the day before and went home drunk and raised a row with his family. He drove them away from home, then went to the barn and slept all night. Coming to the house for breakfast, he and his wife had some words, in which she said she intended to move back to town, as he had promised her he would not drink any more if she married him. He arose from the table, saying "I will settle this," and picking up his revolver, a 32-caliber British bull-dog pattern, stepped to the porch and in the presence of his family and his son-in-law, David Shoemaker, placed the revolver to his right temple and fired, the bullet penetrating his brain. He lingered until 9:30 a. m., when he died. The result is what has been expected, as he had often threatened to preform such an act.

He was a brother by adoption to Mrs. John Kiser, who lived here until recently, and was worth about $50,000.

IMAGE SOURCE: THE HUNTINGTON DEMOCRAT, JULY 17, 1890.

family members were shocked, as Jonas had often threatened to commit suicide.

Indiana newspapers, including those in Indianapolis, Columbus, Fort Wayne, Huntington, and South Bend, covered Jonas' death. The Indianapolis afternoon paper reported the story within hours after his demise.

In the 19th century where guns were a daily part of life, rural communities experienced many deaths by suicide. Most life stories were complicated, and Jonas Baker was no exception. Seventeen years after Jonas's violent death by his hand, historian Samuel P. Kaler offered this tribute, failing to mention the circumstances of Jonas's death.[61]

> He (Jonas Baker) bought land, cleared, and otherwise improved a good farm and became a substantial and praiseworthy citizen, dying on the place which he redeemed from the wilderness in the year 1839.

> Jonas Baker was a man of excellent parts, successful in his business affairs, and at one time the owner of 500 acres of valuable real estate in the county of Whitley. He served several terms as a trustee of Washington Township, was keenly interested in all enterprises for the benefit of the public and stood high in his fellow mans' (sic) esteem and confidence.[62]

How the Long children reacted to their grandfather's death is not known. All three of the Long children knew their Baker grandparents whose farm was a mile or two away. Over and above the highly publicized suicide of their grandfather, the Long children suffered multiple childhood losses, deep wounds rarely discussed.

TOMBSTONE OF JONAS BAKER, EBERHARD CEMETERY. FAMILY PHOTO.

[61] Kaler, Samuel P., and Richard H. Maring, "History of Whitley County, Indiana," Indianapolis, Indiana: B.F. Bowen & Co., 1907, page 708.
[62] Kaler, Samuel P., and Richard H. Maring, "History of Whitley County, Indiana," Indianapolis, Indiana: B.F. Bowen & Co., 1907, page 708.

Amy McVay Abbott

17 The Deadly Woods

Brothers Frank Long and Calvin Long often felled trees on the farm for the Long family's timber business.

Less than two years apart, the brothers frequently worked on the farm together. They had been schooled in everything from raising livestock to using an ax by their father, Washington. The two had been working together in the woods, chopping trees since they were teenagers, with an easy and comfortable relationship between them. The brothers looked out for each other's safety and felled a substantial number of hardwood trees, walnut, elm, oak, and maple.

THE TIMBER BUSINESS WAS KEY TO THE SUCCESS OF THE LONG FARM. A TEAM OF HORSES REMOVES LOGS FROM THE WOOD, ABOUT 1900. FAMILY PHOTO.

As the population of Indiana increased, so did the demand for timber. The need for homes, barns, fence rails, and cords for heating and cooking kept the Long brothers busy with an ax.

In 1800, before pioneers filled all the empty spaces, the forests where Indiana would become the Hoosier State were vast and more than 19.5 million acres. A century later, Indiana had less than 5 million acres of forests.[63]

Diminishing forests were the reality in Indiana. Selling logs to the South Whitley sawmill meant a steady source of income for the Washington Long family. Crops paid off only after harvest.

On Monday, January 18, 1897, Frank and Calvin cut down a large tree in a wooded area. The day was sunny and chilly, with little snow on the ground and no storms forecast in local newspapers.

Frank took a whack at the tree, then Calvin took his ax and cut on the opposite side. Their actions were repeated until the tree trunk was smaller. Neither brother could have anticipated what happened next.

What was left of the tree on the stump split at the base, making a large cracking sound. "This (remaining part of the tree) extended up quite a distance, and as the branches of the falling tree struck others, the resistance was great enough to hurl the entire tree backward and to one side."[64]

Calvin heard the cracking sound and screamed at Frank to get out of the way. He ran toward his brother, frantically moving and flailing his arms. Frank was hard of hearing and didn't initially understand but observed Calvin running and waving his arms.

Calvin was too late. The tree trunk fell on the back of Frank's head, breaking his neck and killing him instantly. Calvin ran back to the barn to get his father and they found Frank's body already cold.[65]

Two days after his death, Frank's funeral was held at Eberhard Lutheran Church, followed by burial in their cemetery. Washington grieved for the rest of his life over the loss of his second son. His firstborn, Willie, had

---

[63] Data on file with the Indiana Department of Natural Resources-Division of Forestry, Indianapolis, Indiana.
[64] "Killed by a Falling Tree," Frank Long, of Washington Township, Meets Death in the Woods, *The Post*, Columbia City, Indiana, Wednesday, January 20, 1897.
[65] "Under a Tree: Frank Long, Washington Township, Comes to an Untimely End," *The Post*, Columbia City, Indiana, Tuesday, January 19, 1897.

died at birth before Frank was born. Another child, daughter Ida died at six months old.

Calvin did not stay in Washington Township but married Elizabeth Huffman and moved to Cleveland Township to raise his family.

Anna was a teenager when her oldest brother died, and she always missed him. No matter who went to the woods, Anna would worry about their safety. Timber clearing and hauling methods improved with new technology, but Anna never forgot the horrible day Frank died. Anna's life was about to change again, as she became of age and young men came calling.

Amy McVay Abbott

18 Anna's New Beau

Washington Long's daughter Anna was a catch for any lucky groom. Anna was popular with friends and neighbors. She had a beautiful countenance, classic facial features around her eyes, orbs that changed color, depending on her mood. No one was ever certain of her eye color; they flashed a gleaming blue when she was laughing or angry or a more mellow green when she was serene. She had a small frame, but her congenial personality drew people to her.

Washington's farm was doing well, and Albina wanted her daughter to dress in the latest fashions. The family occasionally went to Fort Wayne to shop in department and millinery stores where spectacular hats and furs were all the rage in the 1890s. Albina and Anna loved going to the fine millinery stores to check out the latest in hats. Fashionable women selected hats by season and anticipated New York lines, even in tiny Whitley County, Indiana.

ANNA LONG IN A STUDIO PORTRAIT IN THE 1890S. FAMILY PHOTO.

"The openwork straws which had been fashionable in the 1880s continued to be worn in the 1890s. Straw, chip, velvet, and felt were the chief materials used for hats and bonnets but, for the lighter summer millinery, net, chiffon, and lace were often used. Flowers were still used in large quantities for trimming: Hats

89

continue to look like flower-gardens. Violets were particularly fashionable in 1890, and bunches of currants were another favorite trimming of this year. Throughout the decade, there was a fashion for a single high ornament in the trimming, an aigrette of lace or ribbon, a high cock's feather, or one or two ostrich plumes."[66]

KELLIS HOARD IN A STUDIO PORTRAIT TAKEN IN THE 1890S. FAMILY PHOTO.

Anna visited photographers in South Whitley and Columbia City to pose in various outfits during her teenage years, the portraits almost always highlighted by unique hats.

No definitive record tells how Anna met her future husband, Henry Kellis Hoard, who went by his middle name, Kellis. He was the grandson of one of Whitley County's leading citizens, Christian Henry Creager, on his mother Kate's side. Kellis was born in a log cabin in Richland Township on March 1, 1870, somewhere near the village of Lorane. Kate Hoard died when Kellis was 15. When his father could no longer provide for his large family, Kellis lived with the Squire James Grant family in Lorane until age 21. He moved to Cleveland Township to work on the farm of Jonas Kinsey, east of South Whitley. Several of Kellis's siblings lived near South Whitley. He was incredibly close to his oldest sister, Myrta Elva Hoard, who married Jesse Arnold Glassley, owner of the Glassley Department Store, in 1896. On the east side of State Street between Columbia and Front, the Glassley store became a popular place for shopping and visiting.

Kellis married Anna Long on November 16, 1898, at Washington and Albina Long's home farm, the same 160 acres purchased by Reuben Long in 1837. Before their wedding day, Kellis and Anna visited the South Whitley studios of Frank Kelly for portraits, one in travel clothes, and another in their wedding finery. Oliver Frank Kelly became a

DIRECTORY OF SOUTH WHITLEY

The Glassley Dry Goods Company
SOUTH WHITLEY, IND.

Dry Goods,
Clothing, Boots
and Shoes, Ladies
and Gents Furnishings.

In fact everything kept in a first-class store Best goods and lowest prices

SOUTH WHITLEY, IND.

---

[66] "Victorian Hat History: Bonnets, Hats, Caps 1830-1890s." Vintage Dancer. The Vintage Dancer, https://vintagedancer.com/victorian/victorian-hat-history/.

well-known photographer in northeastern Indiana and his work is still prized today, including a large collection at the Indiana Historical Society.

The couple acquired 40 acres from Washington Long north of his original farm and closer to Tunker. Neighbors helped the couple build a house on their new land. In 1902, the Hoards built a large barn that stood for nearly 90 years, from the farm's good hardwood. The interior structural beams still retained the bark of the farm's hardwood trees, walnut, maple, and oak.

KELLIS HOARD WITH A TEAM OF ONE HORSE AND TWO MULES, BEFORE 1900. FAMILY PHOTO.

Kellis often worked with Washington, as they supported each other on their farms. Workdays were long, especially during planting and harvest seasons. At the turn of the new century, horses still played an integral role in fieldwork. When the work in the field was done, horses needed care and feeding before their human caregivers could rest. Washington was grateful for Kellis's work ethic and help.

19 Daughters, Not Sons

Within a year, Kellis and Anna had their first daughter whom they named Zoe Trucia. In 1902, their second daughter Sarah Mae Hoard arrived.

Their house and barn were a short walk to Washington and Albina's home, up the hill across Sugar Creek. When the creek was low in the summer, the girls loved running up the hill to see their grandparents. Ordinarily, they would have had to walk across the bridge on Tunker Road.

Kellis's grandfather Christian Henry Creager died May 20, 1906, at his home in Thorncreek Township where he lived with his son Samuel. Christian had developed dropsy[67] several months before but was still mobile and visited with friends and family almost every day. On the day of his death, he asked for a bowl of milk and some bread. His visitor, a neighbor, went to the kitchen for the snack. When the neighbor returned, Christian's head had fallen back, and he was dead. His funeral was held at the Methodist Episcopal Church in South Whitley, followed by burial in the South Whitley Cemetery.

To the Hoard family's surprise, LeNore Alice Hoard was born in 1908, six years after Mae and nine years after Zoe.

---

[67] Congestive heart failure, causing edema.

DEATH CAME UNHERALDED

AGED PIONEER QUICKLY AN-SWERS FINAL SUMMONS.

While Conversing With Neighbor Christian H. Creager Passed Away At Home Of His Son.

Christian H. Creager, one of the first settlers of Whitley county, laid down life's burden Sunday evening and passed quietly away at seven o'clock at the home of his son, Samuel, in Thorncreek township.

The old gentleman was perhaps as well, if not better, known than any other pioneer in the county, from the fact that he would have been a resident here for seventy years, had he lived until next October.

Although a powerfully built, rugged man, his health began to decline about six months ago when he was attacked by dropsy and the complications attending that disease. For the past five or six weeks he was compelled to sit up in a chair, instead of resting in bed at night, as to lie down affected his heart action. He was able to walk about until the day of his death. He was feeling especially bright and talkative Sunday and a number of people visited him. A short time before his death he called for a bowl of bread and milk and was conversing with a neighbor when his head fell back. Before they could reach his side life was extinct.

His parents were natives of Maryland, but they moved to Montgomery county, Ohio, in 1812, and the deceased was born August 16, 1821, being 84 years, 9 months and 4 days old at the time of his death. He was one of a family of twelve children and came to Cleveland township with his parents in 1836, when the roads were mere Indian trails and almost impassable from mud. On their way to this point they were obliged to abandon one wagon in the north part of Huntington county and the deceased in seeking for help, lost his way in the woods and spent his first night in this county in the open air, without even a fire, and with two inches of snow on the ground. He worked out for fifteen years and then purchased what is now the Wetzel farm, near South Whitley, and operated a saw mill and also ground corn with an old water mill for the incoming settlers. He cut the first stick of timber where South Whitley now stands on the site of the present M. E. church. He was a power in building up the township and his open hearted, charitable nature was always in evidence.

In 1860 he was elected county commissioner and re-elected three years later, being the only candidate elected on the democratic ticket. During the war he assisted many families through the privations of that period, caused by the absence of husbands and sons who were enlisted and his good deeds have never been forgotten.

In 1840 he married Susanna Obenchain who died in 1862. Seven children were born to them, five surviving as follows: Samuel, of Thorncreek; John, of Cleveland townships; and Riley Creager, of Beaumont, Texas; Mrs. Peter Hess, of Thorncreek township, and Mrs. George Ream, of Larwill.

In 1863 he married Mrs. Elizabeth Mettler and she died about ten years ago. To this union four children were born all living as follows: Joseph of Elkhart; Angeline, of Ft. Wayne; Oscar B., of Columbia township, and Mrs. Armenta Kline, near Barbee Lake. In addition to his own children three daughters of his second wife, to whom he was a father also survive: Mrs. Emil Doriot, of this city; Mrs. Samuel Mettert of Goshen and Mrs. Pete Brown, of Michigan City. Twenty-seven grand children and twenty-two great grand children are also among his descendants.

Of all the family of the twelve original Creager children, he is the last but one, John Creager, of West Manchester, Ohio, still surviving.

FUNERAL OCCURS WEDNESDAY.

Six grandsons and two great grandsons will act as the pall bearers. They are as follows: George Ream, Jr., of Larwill; Roy Creager, of Kendallville; Charles Hoard and Archie Hoard, of Washington township; Walter Creager, of Cleveland township; J. E. Hess, of Thorncreek township; Ray Glassley, of this city and Carl Keirn, of Thorncreek township. The latter two are great grandsons.

The funeral cortege will leave the Creager residence at 9 a. m. Wednesday for the M. E. church at South Whitley and the last services will be performed on arrival, Rev. Ernest E. Lutes officiating; interment in South Whitley cemetery.

PHOTO CAPTION: THE CREAGER BROTHERS WERE PHOTOGRAPHED TOGETHER SOMETIME AFTER THE TURN OF THE CENTURY. LEFT TO RIGHT: JOHN (DIED 1908), LEVI (DIED 1907), AND CHRISTIAN (DIED 1906).

NEWSPAPER CAPTION: SOUTH WHITLEY TRIBUNE, AUGUST 23, 1906.

Family life centered around the farm. Anna taught the older girls everything she knew about housekeeping, and by their early teens, both Zoe and Mae were proficient in running the home.

The family kept a dairy cow for their own needs. Anna milked the cow twice a day, putting on her sunbonnet to avoid the sun's harshness. She taught her daughters to run the milk separator, an apparatus with a large and ugly bowl on top. Anna poured the milk into the bowl, and the machine separated it, cream out one chute, and skim milk out the other. The cream might be kept for family use or sold to a neighbor. The hogs and calves were the beneficiaries of the skim milk.

Anna taught Zoe and Mae how to use the square wooden butter churn to make homemade butter. She was also proficient in making cottage cheese.

જે

Kellis loved all his daughters, but he spent much time joking and laughing with LeNore, whom he called "Teeter." What did the nickname mean? From babyhood on, LeNore was moody, silly, creative, and funny. She was loud and boisterous, with an up and down temperament. Was her father referring to her as a teeter-totter?

Everyone except her father called her LeNore, her given name. Kellis named her after his Aunt LeNore Hoard Allen, an elegant woman married to an Indianapolis physician. LeNore stayed close to Aunt LeNore and Uncle Ethan's daughter Helene Allen McLaughlin.

As LeNore grew, she played more and spent time with Mae. LeNore and Zoe both had strong personalities, and Mae was their balm. Zoe and LeNore might be called "high maintenance" in the parlance of today. Mae had a softer personality, more like her mother.

The three girls had an ordinary rural childhood, enjoying the beauty of the farm. Grandpa Long often hitched a team to his snow sleigh when the weather was right, taking the grandchildren on a sleigh ride down Tunker Road and around the section.

SOUVENIR BOOKLET FROM ZOE HOARD'S FIRST GRADE YEAR, TUNKER SCHOOL, 1905.
IMAGE COURTESY SOUTH WHITLEY COMMUNITY PUBLIC LIBRARY.

MAE AND LENORE

Grandpa had a set of sleigh bells, which rang with each clip-clop of the horses' hooves on gravel roads.

The children enjoyed skating and sledding, attending school parties and dances, and visiting relatives in Indiana and Illinois.

MAE HOARD WITH HER EIGHTH GRADE CLASSMATES AT THE TUNKER SCHOOL.
BOTTOM ROW (LEFT TO RIGHT): FLO KREIDER, TEACHER CHARLES STONER, TRESSIE TOY KEEL-KITE.
TOP ROW (LEFT TO RIGHT): WELDON GROSS, MAE HOARD, LOIS YODER.

Kellis and Anna occasionally bought treats for their daughters from the wandering huckster wagon, driven by store owner Perry Yoder, who periodically visited, selling everything from sewing needles and tools to hard candy. His visits were a welcome respite from the assigned chores of all three girls. Anna allowed her daughters to select something from the wagon, a new hair ribbon or candy or sweet treats or whatever whim of the day.[68]

❧

Anna and Kellis wanted their three daughters to have more education than they themselves did. Anna always regretted not finishing high school. She had had a love of books ingrained into her by her stepmother Albina. Zoe and Mae were also great readers.

All three girls attended district schools until high school when they attended Washington Center High School and rode a community wagon, known as the hack, the term for a school bus, pulled by a team of horses.

After high school graduation Zoe ventured to Indiana University in Bloomington, later transferring to Manchester College. Attending college, especially a large university 175 miles away, was unusual for girls. Why she didn't go back is unknown, but she finished her education six miles from home at Manchester College.

WASHINGTON CENTER HIGH SCHOOL.
IMAGE COURTESY OF WHITLEY COMMUNITY PUBLIC LIBRARY.

Mae graduated from Washington Center High School two years after her older sister. Mae attended summer workshops for teachers at nearby Manchester College. Requirements to teach were inconsistent, and the

---

[68] "Bought an Auto Truck," *The Journal-Gazette*, Fort Wayne, Indiana, April 11, 1917.

minimum needed was a certified 12-week course from a college or university. Mae became employed by the district schools in Washington Township.

LeNore went to a three-year diploma school to earn her nursing degree at Lutheran Hospital in Fort Wayne. She was accompanied by her lifelong friend Marie Luecke Bridge who also became a nurse. LeNore and Marie remained friends until LeNore's 1994 death.

Kellis and Anna pushed their daughters towards additional education. Unfortunately, that goal existed in direct opposition to another dream, that of family continuing to live on and farm the family land. Each daughter stepped out of her comfort zone and into a broader, more expansive world, that may not have included the Long and Hoard farms in Washington Township.

20 The New Machine

The twentieth century brought a significant change in transportation for Whitley County. The horse and buggy, a ubiquitous site in town and country, would go the way of the log cabin and the spinning wheel. Tractors and trucks retired the family horses. Buggies were relegated to the back of the barn, and most of the horses went to the proverbial glue factory.[69] By 1909, Whitley County automobile agencies had sold about 30 machines, bringing automobiles in the county to about 100.[70]

Most country people called the Ford Model T a machine. The mass-produced automobile was first for sale in 1908. Inventor Henry Ford was the first to use an assembly line in large-scale manufacturing, keeping the price low enough for the average man to purchase.

Between 1913 and 1927, Ford produced more than 15 million machines.[71] By 1920, nearly half of the United States cars were Model Ts, also known as the "Tin Lizzie."[72]

Washington Long was determined to get a machine of his own. The car was so popular that many Indiana dealers had a waiting list. Washington bought a train ticket to Detroit and headed to the automotive plant.

---

[69] "Bipartisan Bill Introduced in Congress to End Slaughter of American Equines." *A Humane World,* February 5, 2019. https://blog.humanesociety.org/2019/01/bipartisan-bill-introduced-in-congress-to-end-slaughter-of-american-equines.html.

[70] "Fifty Years Ago, *The Commercial-Mail,* Columbia City, Indiana, November 21, 1959.

[71] History.com Editors. "Model T." History.com. A& E Television Networks, April 26, 2010. https://www.history.com/topics/inventions/model-t.

[72] Krigsman, Amy. "History of the Ford Dealership in America." Car Life Nation, November 25, 2019. https://carlifenation.com/history-of-the-ford-dealership-in-america.

A family member took Washington to the New York, Chicago & St. Louis Railroad (called the Nickel Plate Railroad) depot in South Whitley to board his train. South Whitley had numerous railroads running through at all hours of the day and night. Passenger trains frequently stopped at the depot; those heading east might go to Buffalo, New York, or Cincinnati to catch another east-bound train. Trains going west traveled to Chicago.

P0269_G_5X7_BOX5_050

SOUTH WHITLEY TRAIN DEPOT, 1912, IMAGE BY O. FRANK KELLY,
INDIANA HISTORICAL SOCIETY P0269

Washington boarded the train in his finest suit. As a frequent train traveler, he always dressed to the nines looking every bit the country gentleman. He changed trains at Toledo, with no direct routes to Detroit available from northeastern Indiana. He went to the River Rouge plant and learned that they did not sell the machines directly to consumers. However, they directed him to a local Michigan dealer. Detroit dealers were flush with hot-off-the-assembly line machines and sold them to walk-ins from all over the Midwest.

The average cost for a Model T was around $850, but it could rise to nearly two grand with accoutrements. Millions of Fords would be made at the famous plant, including the iconic Mustang, decades later.

Washington's drive home to Tunker from south of Detroit—200 miles—would have taken hours in the late 1910s. Model T tires weren't much more than rigged-up bicycle tires, and even the main roads were often unpaved.

Anna was worried about her father after he had been gone a couple of days. He had little experience with cars, having test-driven a neighbor's machine. She went to sit with her stepmother, Albina, and wait for her father to come home. Anna wasn't sure how long he would be gone, two days? Five days? As soon as the sun dipped below the horizon, she became more concerned and waited outside in the lane, holding a lantern. Anna was unfamiliar with the new machine and didn't know if it had lights.

A buggy out at night might have a lantern or two on its side but cast a far different look than the new Model T. Soon enough, Anna spotted two dim lights coming south on the Tunker Road. The lights sat much lower than a buggy lantern. Closer and closer, the lights moved toward her until she saw them coming at her on the lane. It was her father in his new car who shouted to his daughter, "Annie, you didn't think they would make these things without lights, did you?"

The machine, which the family called Old Henry, had a new home in the barn with Washington's horses.

ZOE (IN BLACK HAT) AND HER FRIENDS VISIT THE SOUTH WHITLEY FESTIVAL ON A FALL AFTERNOON IN GRANDPA LONG'S CAR. FAMILY PHOTO.

Washington was generous with his vehicles and let his older granddaughters drive when they were teenagers. Kellis purchased a four-door model T after Washington bought his two-door. Eventually, the horses made the fabled trip to the glue factory, replaced by gasoline-powered equipment. Now Washington and Kellis could use feed for other animals but had to purchase gasoline for their vehicles.

Tractors soon became available, but they had steel wheels with lugs, unlike today's models. These tractors could only be used in the fields; if a farmer took his tractor on the roads, the spikey lugs put huge holes in the road.

KELLIS AND DOG POSING AT THE FARM WITH HIS FORD. FAMILY PHOTO.

At age 12, LeNore decided she wanted to drive Old Henry. Why not? Grandpa trusted both of her sisters to drive his machine. Never mind, they were six and nine years older. LeNore however, was a tall child, so her feet could reach the pedals. LeNore had supreme confidence that she could do anything from infancy, and what's more, knew all about it.

She took off from the farm in the machine, headed towards Columbia City. Distracted, LeNore drove into a ditch, turning the car upside down. For the adolescent, losing control was easy on a lovely summer day when one hasn't the foggiest notion of how to drive. Later, she would point out to grandchildren the spot where she turned over in the ditch. As her father might say, that was Teeter being Teeter.

104

21 Threshing Day

LeNore detested rising early and fought like the devil to stay undisturbed in bed. Teeter, the baby of the family, received privileges not given to her sisters, especially from her father. She sometimes slept late, avoiding morning chores.

Not today. LeNore was the first one awake in the household this summer day, well before her sisters and parents. Only the rooster was up before the eight-year-old. Today was the threshing day at the Hoard farm, a magical once-a-year event everyone anticipated.

LeNore awakened her parents in the big bedroom on the main floor. She dressed and was outside as the sun rose over the woods, a golden sparkle above a darkened blanket of trees. Dawn arrived to greet a beautiful summer day on the farm, wildflowers waking in attention toward the sun, the last of the milkweed pods ebbing and flowing in the slight breeze. What child can resist picking a milkweed plant and blowing the feathery seeds to skip and fly away into the air?

LeNore was delighted. Even on the hottest of summer days, neighbors came in droves to help, bringing most of LeNore's cousins and playmates. Today would be a good day, with friends and cousins from South Whitley, excitement, and plenty of good food.

Kellis planted his winter wheat crop in autumn, and by mid-summer the stalks had ripened. He and his hired man cut and bound the harvest with a reaper binder pulled by his team of horses. The machine bound the wheat stems to make bundles. Also called sheaves, these bundles were shaped into cones, resembling tiny teepees. Kellis left his grain in the field to dry, and with neighbors who also reaped and bound their crop, started a threshing ring.[73]

There were few easy jobs on the Long farm on threshing day. Farmers hitched their best teams to a wagon and came to the Hoard farm with their entire family. Everyone stayed until the work was finished. Most, except for the babies and smallest children, had a job. Mae and Zoe had kitchen duty with their mother, but LeNore had only one assignment later in the day.

Kellis kept his team in the barn the neighbors had helped build, an imposing structure with walnut and oak bark-covered rafter beams made from the woods on his father-in-law's farm.

P0269_G_5X7_BOX14_151

WHITLEY COUNTY THRESHING RING MACHINERY AND CREW. IMAGE BY O. FRANK KELLY, INDIANA HISTORICAL SOCIETY P0269

Threshing day was a chance to show off to the neighbors. Farmers oiled horse harnesses to shine in the sun and spit-polished brass fittings. Anna peeked out a south-facing window and smiled with pride at the sight of her husband harnessing his team of white draft horses, dazzlingly bright against the diffuse morning sun.

---

[73] "South Whitley News," *The Journal-Gazette*, Fort Wayne, Indiana, February 20, 1918.

The farm on a July morning looked like a painting—the shocks of wheat, standing upright in the field ready for the threshers. In the distance between the wheat fields and the woods, stood green, shoulder-high corn, tassels waving slightly in the morning breeze. Wildflowers on every bank, fallow hill, and nook and cranny, stretched for morning light.

Neighbors arrived in their wagons with their own horses' harnesses gleaming. LeNore stood at the end of the lane, waving at the arriving neighbors and their children.

Emmet Miller, Ervin Pook, Fred Keymeyer, Charles Hunter, and Kellis had organized the Red River Threshing Company for their area. The threshing ring came with a crew and a threshing machine, a loud, sputtering, oversized steam engine pulled by horses. Teams traveled from farm to farm; neighbors worked as partners because no one could do the labor-intensive work by himself. The group erected a building on Emmet Miller's property to house the large equipment.[74]

Horse-drawn wagons brought the bundled shocks to the threshing machine. The process was slow-going. The crew put the wheat through the thresher, separating the grain from the straw. Kellis and Anna could not have harvested on their farm without neighbors' assistance. The next day, the same crews moved due north across Sugar Creek to Washington Long's farm. Kellis, Anna, the girls, and the Hoards' hired man would help their neighbors, as they had been helped.

Straw, which served both as animal feed and bedding, went into the big barn's haymow. The grain was prepared for sale. Kellis would later transport it by wagonload to the Farmer's Elevator in South Whitley, where he served as a director.

Inside the house and in the nearby summer kitchen, the womenfolk prepared the meals, a small lunch at midmorning, a large dinner at noon, and supper at about 4 p.m. The women killed chickens by tying their feet to an iron fence that enclosed the Hoards' apple orchard. Zoe took an ax and chopped off the broilers' heads. Zoe and Mae had become proficient at killing chickens, watching their mother and grandmother Albina Long do it many times. Chicken blood drained onto the ground.

Many hands made light work of pulling off all the feathers and removing the inedible innards. What remained after the feather-plucking was thrown into a vat of boiling water dragged from the summer kitchen, a

---

[74] "South Whitley News," *The Journal-Gazette*, Fort Wayne, Indiana, February 20, 1918.

screened room outside the main house. The roasters were cut in pieces, dipped in flour or cornmeal batter, then fried in lard.

Sawhorses, with boards to make tables, were placed under shade trees near the house for meals. The meals featured the fried chicken, salted ham, roast beef, mashed potatoes and gravy, a bounty of canned and fresh vegetables, desserts, cakes, and pies to energize the workers for another shift in the field.

Before the meal, Anna Hoard made sure every worker washed his hands at a large washing basin near the summer kitchen.[75]

Youngsters played in the yard, avoiding the fields unless sent by an adult on an errand. Children jumped from ropes tied around a beam in the haymow onto the barn's wooden floor. Older boys often rode a pony to carry water to the fields, while older girls were given errands from the women or promoted to the kitchen.

LeNore had one job. Anna asked her youngest daughter to make and take lemonade to the workers in the field. Anna gave her a bucket and a scoop. LeNore added water, sugar, and lemon juice to the bucket, with a good amount of ice. In a moment of poor judgment or long-planned escapade, she added Epsom salts to her concoction. With many cousins the same age, LeNore may have had a partner in the crime. If a collaborator existed, he or she escaped detection.

Epsom salts, or magnesium sulfate, were widely used for many ailments. Farmers used it to make a poultice when an animal had an injury. Farm wives added a little around the base of garden plants. The salts were never intended for human consumption because of a sobering side effect, almost immediate diarrhea.

LeNore walked along the edge of the field, motioning to invite the men to enjoy a cold drink. Within minutes the lemonade hit the threshers' intestines, and all hell broke loose. The workers headed for the woods. The farm had one lone privy, near the garden, too far for the supreme urgency of the moment.

The deed was done. The child, who loved attention, attracted notoriety. The Hoards' youngest daughter had slowed the threshing process, an act that may have raised the ire of the helpful neighbors.

---

75 Telephone Conversation, Donna Enz Argon, Bedford, Massachusetts, and author, April 10, 2016.

22 Clans and Community Celebrations

In the early 1900s, 175 family members traveled by horse and buggy to a reunion at the Hoard farm. Members of the Creager family (Kellis's mother's family) gathered for an annual reunion.

CREAGER FAMILY REUNION, FARM OF KELLIS AND ANNA LONG HOARD, TUNKER, INDIANA, 1902. FAMILY PHOTO.

In 1906 when Kellis and Anna hosted the reunion, the barn lot overflowed with buggies belonging to cousins across the state. Relatives came from the towns of Huntington, North Manchester, Kendallville, and Michigan City.

The family served a large dinner on make-shift tables set on the lawn. After lunch, the reunion chair, Charles W. Alexander of Washington Township, called the program to order. Creager cousins entertained with songs and dances, and a speaker talked on a patriotic subject. Alexander read a list of new marriages, new babies, and then the sad list of those who passed. In 1906, at the Hoard home, a long tableau honored Christian Henry Creager who had passed in Thorncreek Township two months before.

Alexander was re-elected as chair for 1907, with Miss Lila Burwell of Cleveland Township re-elected as secretary for the following year. The next reunion was slated for September 1907 at the North Manchester fairgrounds.[76]

Kellis and Anna hosted the 21st annual reunion in 1922 when Kellis served as president of the Creager Reunion Committee with Oscar Banfill Creager, vice president; Howard Creager, treasurer; and Florence Glassley, secretary.

Three hundred people attended and enjoyed music by an orchestra trio from South Whitley composed of Miss Beulah Baldwin, Herbert Harley, and Keith Glassley. The Indiana Herald reported, "A program of recitations, games, and music was enjoyed, and a basket dinner was served."[77]

WASHINGTON AND ALBINA LONG HOSTED A REUNION OF THE LONG FAMILY ANNUALLY. INCLUDED IN THIS 1916 PICTURE (LEFT TO RIGHT): BERYL LONG, LENORE HOARD, UNKNOWN, MAE HOARD, UNKNOWN, UNKNOWN, UNKNOWN, ANNA LONG HOARD, ZOE HOARD, WASHINGTON LONG, UNKNOWN, UNKNOWN, ALBINA LONG, CALVIN LONG, 2 UNKNOWN MEN. FAMILY PHOTO.

---

[76] "Creager Families Hold Big Reunion Sunday." *The Daily-News Democrat,* Huntington, Indiana, September 17, 1906.
[77] "Creager Reunion." *The Indiana Herald*, Huntington, Indiana, August 8, 1922.

The Long family also had reunions but not as often as the Creagers. Washington and Albina hosted the family at their home, and Anna and Kellis helped with the preparation and tear-down. By the turn of the century, Washington and his sister Sarah Weybright were the only living children of Reuben and Elizabeth Long. Jacob Long had died in 1879, and Catherine Long Obenchain passed away in 1893. Sarah would die shortly after the new century arrived, in 1902.

❧

Serving the community was a family tradition. Kellis's grandfather Christian Creager had been a county commissioner several times, as had his father-in-law Washington Long. Kellis identified as a Democrat but kept his service primarily to agriculture organizations, which supported his land passion.

In 1912, farmers in South Whitley and area townships met to talk about starting a grain elevator. One-hundred and forty men started the Farmers' Equity Union to build the elevator as soon as the weather cleared.[78] The group intended to build a functional elevator by the time harvest rolled around in the fall.

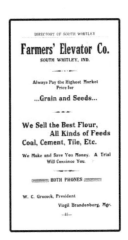

ADVERTISEMENT FROM SOUTH WHITLEY CITY DIRECTOR FOR FARMERS' ELEVATOR. DATE UNKNOWN.

Kellis was elected secretary of the incorporated group. Other officers included: Lewis Mishler, president; Bob Domer, vice president; John Swihart, treasurer; and Frank Huffman, fifth member.

The Farmers' Elevator would become a prominent landmark in South Whitley and a hub for farmers who now had a place to sell grain that didn't require excess travel. A site was selected between the Vandalia and the Nickel Plate railroad tracks on the north side of South Whitley where, more than a century later, the business still exists. Before a shovel of dirt was scooped, the active group had raised $6,000 in stock.

---

[78] "Equity Union Over at South Whitley." *The Indiana Herald*, Huntington, Indiana, March 4, 1912.

23 Enemies Seen and Unseen

Albina Long became paralyzed and bed-bound after suffering a stroke in early 1917. With the family's help, Washington took loving care of her, though it broke his heart. Just days after a second, more devastating stroke, Albina died in June at their home near Sugar Creek. She and Washington had been married for nearly 37 years. Albina had no children of her own and had become a mother to Washington's children and grandmother to his grandchildren. She would be missed.

Americans entered the Great War—a contemporaneous name for World War I—in April 1917, two months after the U.S. broke off formal relations with Germany. The Selective Service Act, passed in spring 1917, called for three rounds of conscription of all U.S. men, ages 18 to 45. Ultimately, three million American soldiers served in World War I. Many Whitley County boys were "over there," as memorialized in a popular song by George M. Cohen during the war.[79]

Farmers were encouraged to grow excess crops as their contribution to the war effort. Ultimately, many families contributed the flesh and blood of their sons, brothers, and friends.

Families grew large gardens for fresh food. Women and girls canned extensively, using the Indiana-made Ball glass jars. The Hoards' garden stood east of the summer kitchen, where Anna canned vegetables and cleaned chickens.

---

[79] Rosenberg, Jennifer. "The Story Behind the Famous World War I Song 'Over There'." ThoughtCo. Accessed April 3, 2021. https://www.thoughtco.com/over-there-song-1779207.

A smokehouse stood nearby, where Kellis hung hams to cure and occasionally hung sausage made in the summer kitchen. Anna also kept bees, the hives located near the pollen-rich garden. One of the Maiden-Blush apple trees from the previous century remained. The tree held the clothesline, attached to an iron post on the opposite end.

❧

A more insidious enemy reared its ugly head during the winter months. The Spanish flu—likely misnamed—crossed to humans from hogs on a central U.S. farm. Influenza raced through the military, in the States and on the war front. By 1920, the disease killed millions worldwide, civilian and military.

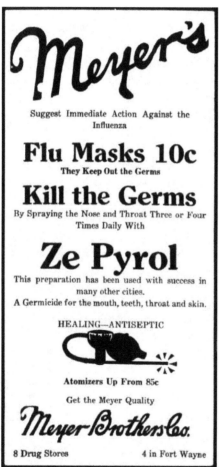

Fort Wayne Sentinel,
Wednesday, December 4, 1918

In 1918's early months, Whitley County saw few influenza cases but always had some typhoid cases on the Health Department's books. Cases in Indiana dropped off as summer came and people went on with their lives.

On Wednesday, May 15, 1918, Anna was at the Dunkard Church attending a Red Cross meeting around noon. Some of the local women knitted sweaters for soldiers, while others made bandages for the wounded in Europe. The women talked about their lives—the war, local boys who enlisted, and the outbreaks of cholera, typhoid, and influenza.

Mae, 18, was frying ham and eggs on the wood stove in the farmhouse kitchen. Zoe and LeNore had gone up the hill to Grandpa Long's house for a visit, and Kellis was in a neighbor's field, helping him plant corn.[80]

---

[80] "Farm Home Burns." *Fort Wayne Sentinel.*, Fort Wayne, Indiana, May 16, 1918.

114

A man passing by on the Tunker Road saw flames coming out of the Hoard farmhouse's top floor. He went to the door and found Mae, who was unaware of the fire. The man went for help, and Mae called the local telephone operator who sounded the fire alarm, which alerted the neighbors by ringing a particular alarm on their phones.

"There was no fire department back then," LeNore Hoard Enz told a journalist nearly 60 years later.[81]

The fire burned the house to the ground, but not before family and neighbors could remove a few things, including a rolltop desk. All but one of the maple trees that surrounded the Hoard home burned. Using a gasoline engine pump to spray water, a neighbor saved the summer kitchen, which was east of the house.

LeNore recalled her father wept at the sight of his burned home. "I remember crying because my doll, one with long black hair Mama ordered from a Sears and Roebuck catalog, was afire upstairs."[82]

Thankfully, Kellis and Anna were insured by Farmers Mutual and built a new home on the old foundation. The new house was a Cape Cod style with a wide front porch. A large living room, kitchen, and dining room filled the first floor. The dining room space included a large window that looked north to Grandpa Long's farm and Sugar Creek. The family added space for a lavatory and large bedroom also on the first floor. Those who slept upstairs still had to use a chamber pot or go downstairs in the middle of the night.

Only one radiator generated heat for the entire house, in the big downstairs living room, and upstairs had a lone 10-inch register for the entire floor. The kitchen still had a wood stove, and the furnace burned both coal and wood. In the winter, the family spent much time in the kitchen to enjoy the heat.[83]

The kitchen featured a large built-in cabinet, called "Grandma Hoard's cabinet," which had a secret back door to the bedroom and could hold a child wanting to hide or play a trick.

---

81 "Snowbird Shares Pioneer History," Heritage 1776 Series. *The Clearwater Sun*, Clearwater, Florida, April 25, 1976.
82 "Snowbird Shares Pioneer History," Heritage 1778 Series, *The Clearwater Sun*, Clearwater, Florida, April 25, 1976.
83 Telephone conversation with Donna Enz Argon, April 10, 2016.

The upstairs had three rooms, a large central area and two small bedrooms. This level's unusual item was the tank room, filled with a large metal water tank, a safety measure that didn't come from an insurance company. Kellis formulated the idea, wanting to protect his daughters who slept upstairs. In case of a fire, gallons of water would be right there to pour on the flames.

Night was a peaceful and pleasant time for anyone who slept upstairs, which often included one of Kellis's siblings or family members. The sounds of a country night, a far distant locomotive, a hooting barn owl, or breeze rippling through the apple orchard, lulled one to sleep.

The new house was built on the original foundation, so the same cellar served the family. The rooms near the cellar stairs were for food storage and washing and crating eggs. The cream separator and wringer washing machine were also kept there. When Anna got a gasoline-powered washing machine, it was housed in the summer kitchen, convenient to the clothesline. In winter, Anna used her washing machine in the cellar. The cellar's backroom had an outside entrance for the wood and coal needed to run the furnace and stove. The basement didn't freeze in the winter and stayed cool in the summer.[84]

LeNore was ten when the new house was built, young enough her two older sisters could play tricks on her. Zoe and Mae told LeNore the upstairs had a ghost. Zoe and Mae convinced their gullible younger sister that their Uncle Frank—dead since before all were born—haunted the upstairs and made his shoes walk from the tank room to LeNore's bedroom.

Uncle Frank Long, Anna's brother who had died in a farm accident in 1897, could not have kept his shoes at the Hoard home because it wasn't built until after his death. And had he left them there by some time transference miracle, his shoes would have burned in the 1918 fire. Yet, the legend lived on to torment LeNore. She told it to her children and grandchildren, who were always looking for Uncle Frankie's shoes.

❧

The second wave of the Spanish flu came to Indiana in the fall, with a vengeance unseen in its first wave. By the end of September, the Indiana State Board of Health had closed most Indiana schools. On Wednesday, October 23, 1918, *The Herald Press* story proclaimed, "Flu is Spreading:

---

[84] Telephone conversation with Donna Enz Argon and author, March 5, 2016.

Ban May Remain On." In addition to closing schools, the health commissioners closed public meetings and churches.[85]

The Great War ended when the Armistice was signed on November 11, 1918, a temporary peace between the Allies and the Germans. After several extensions, the Treaty of Versailles was signed at the French castle a year later. More than 135,000 Hoosiers served in World War I, with more than 3,000 killed during the fighting. Americans hoped the War to End All Wars would be the last global conflict they would see in their lifetimes.

INFLUENZA

How to Avoid It—How to Care for Those Who Have It

The following suggestions of the Indiana State Board of Health may prove of immeasurable value to any man or woman who will read, remember and act upon them in the present great emergency. The counsel here set forth has been prepared after consultation with some of the ablest medical men in America. If you will follow this official bulletin, you will be doing your duty to your fellow man and to yourself.

What To Do Until the Doctor Comes

If you feel a sudden chill, followed by muscular pain, headache, backache, unusual tiredness and fever GO TO BED AT ONCE.

Be sure to have enough bed clothing to keep you warm.

Open all windows in your bedroom and keep them open at all times, except in rainy weather.

Take medicine to open the bowels freely.

Take some nourishing food such as milk, egg-and-milk or broth every four hours.

Stay in bed until a physician tells you that it is safe to get up.

Allow no one else to sleep in the same room.

Protect others by sneezing and coughing into handkerchiefs or cloths, which should be boiled or burned.

Insist that whoever gives you water or food or enters the sick room for any other purpose shall wear a gauze mask, which may be obtained from the Red Cross or may be made at home of four to six folds of gauze and which should cover the nose and mouth and be tied behind the head.

Remember that these masks must be kept clean, must be put on outside the sick room, must not be handled after they are tied on and must be boiled 30 minutes and thoroughly dried every time they are taken off.

To Householders

Keep out of the sick room unless attendance is necessary.

Do not handle articles coming from the sick room until they are boiled.

Allow no visitors, and do not go visiting.

Call a doctor for all inmates who show signs of beginning sickness.

The usual symptoms are: Inflamed and watery eyes, discharging nose, backache, headache, muscular pain, and fever.

Keep away from crowded places, such as "movies," theatres, street cars.

See to it that your children are kept warm and dry, both night and day.

Have sufficient fire in your home to disperse the dampness.

Open your windows at night. If cool weather prevails, add extra bed clothing.

To Workers

Walk to work if possible.

Avoid the person who coughs or sneezes.

Wash your hands before eating.

Make full use of all available sunshine.

Do not use a common towel. It spreads disease.

Should you cough or sneeze, cover nose and mouth with a handkerchief.

Keep out of crowded places. Walk in the open air rather than go to crowded places of amusement.

Sleep is necessary for well-being—avoid over-exertion. Eat good, clean food.

Keep away from houses where there are cases of influenza.

If sick, no matter how slightly, see a physician.

If you have had influenza, stay in bed until your doctor says you can safely get up.

To Nurses

Keep clean. Isolate your patients.

When in attendance upon patients, wear a mask which will cover both the nose and the mouth. When the mask is once in place, do not handle it.

Change the mask every two hours. Owing to the scarcity of gauze, boil for ½ hour and rinse, then use the gauze again.

Wash your hands each time you come in contact with the patient. Use bichloride of mercury, 1-1000, or Liquor Cresol compound, 1-100, for hand disinfection.

Obtain at least seven hours' sleep in each twenty-four hours. Eat plenty of good, clean food.

Walk in the fresh air daily.

Sleep with your windows open.

Insist that the patient cough, sneeze or expectorate into cloths that may be disinfected or burned.

Boil all dishes.

Keep patients warm.

Pocket size folders, reproducing the suggestions embodied in this announcement, may be obtained without charge, for distribution anywhere in Indiana, upon application to the

INDIANA STATE BOARD OF HEALTH

INDIANA STATE BOARD OF HEALTH, IMAGE IN THE PUBLIC DOMAIN.

---

[85] "Flu Is Spreading; Ban May Remain On," *The Herald Press*, Huntington, Indiana, October 23, 1918.

On December 7, Dr. E.V. Nolt, Whitley County Health Officer, announced township trustees could decide their township school's status. Some schools had closed for most of the fall semester. The influenza pandemic of 1918 didn't ramp down until the end of December when Dr. Nolt told *The Journal-Gazette* "the situation is greatly improved."[86] The influenza pandemic, while slowing in December, was not fully resolved for another year.

In November, Grandpa Long traveled by train to Tempe, Arizona, with his son, Calvin, who suffered from tuberculosis. Calvin stayed in a tuberculosis sanitarium with his father nearby. Father and son did not return to Whitley County until the following spring.

WASHINGTON LONG AND HIS SON CALVIN IN TEMPE, ARIZONA, WHERE CALVIN RECEIVED TREATMENT FOR TUBERCULOSIS, 1919. FAMILY PHOTO.

---

[86] Flu Decreases in Whitley County, *The Journal-Gazette*, Fort Wayne, Indiana, December 27, 1918.

24 Music on the Victrola

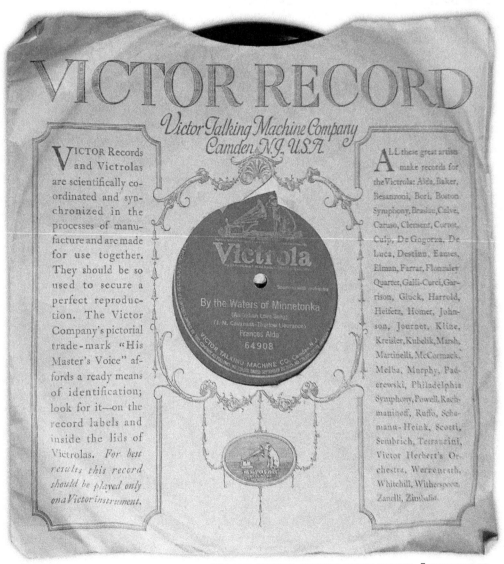

THE HOARD DAUGHTERS OWNED MANY 78S AND ENJOYED HOSTING DANCE PARTIES. FAMILY PHOTO.

Among their collection were 78RPM records by Al Jolson, a white man who sang in blackface to mimic past minstrel shows. In 1919, Jolson had three songs among the top hits, including *Down Where the Suwanee River Flows, On the Road to Calais,* and *Tell that to the Marines.* The top song of 1919 was *After You're Gone* by Marion Harris.

RCA VICTOR VICTROLA
FLOOR MODEL,
PURCHASED AT W.F.
NORRIS REXALL DRUG,
SOUTH WHITLEY, INDIANA
1918. FAMILY PHOTO.

The Victrola was a floor model but lacked bellows like the one on the RCA Victor logo. A hand crank operated the set, and two speakers were in the front, sending the sound through the room.

25 Venus Rising

Two longs—two shorts. Again. Two longs—two shorts.

LeNore woke when she heard the wall phone's distinctive ringer in the kitchen below her bedroom. Like all on a party-line, the Long family had a unique sound assigned to them from the telephone company..

LeNore looked at the clock, 10:00 p.m. Late for a call, she thought. The telephone buzzed until LeNore heard a mumbled voice answer. She drifted back to sleep, the curtains fluttering in the slight breeze of an August night.

LeNore felt someone shake her shoulders. It was Zoe, weeping, trying to awaken her younger sister.

"There's been an accident, LeNore," said Zoe. "Mae's at St. Joe Hospital, and she's hurt. I'm going to the hospital with Mama and Daddy. You sit with Grandpa."

LeNore couldn't believe Mae had had an accident. It hadn't been more than a few hours since Mae left the house with her friends, as LeNore swung on the front porch swing. From the wooden swing, Grandpa Long and LeNore frequently watched cars come over the Tunker Road hill. A soft-top Ford roadster had turned into the driveway, with three young people inside. Mae's friends had picked her up for a Sunday night date to one of Fort Wayne's theaters, The Majestic or The Jefferson. LeNore and Grandpa had walked around the front yard, waving as the group left.

As darkness fell, only a sliver of the moon appeared. Grandpa showed LeNore what his father had taught him, where to find Venus in the sky.

Tonight Venus was not yet visible; only the skinny moon broke the sky of dusk.[87]

Since the beginning of time, farmers watched the skies and the ascent and descent of stars and planets to mark seasons. Venus, named for the Roman goddess of love, was often the brightest orb in the sky and sometimes appeared blue.

KELLIS AND ANNA HOARD AT THEIR HOME WITH THREE DAUGHTERS, MAE, LENORE, AND ZOE, AND KELLIS'S EVER-PRESENT DOG, ABOUT 1919. FAMILY PHOTO.

Earlier in August, Mae had returned home from her second summer of teacher training at Manchester College with her friend, Esther Moyer. Mae had confided in her little sister all about her upcoming evening with Thomas McCoy, arranged by Esther and her date, Lawrence Schrader. Esther was Mae's fellow teacher and played matchmaker for Thomas and Mae after the girls' return home from Manchester College.

---

[87] Ashford, Ade. Almanac v2.0, March 2, 2007. https://skyandtelescope.org/wp-content/plugins/observing-tools/almanac/almanac.html.

McCoy, a farmer from Columbia City, was a year older than Mae. Thomas attracted young ladies' attention with his jet-black curly hair parted in the middle, dark, deep-set eyes, and classic features. Mae was popular; she had a more winning personality than her two gregarious sisters. She was more like her mother, with a soft, round face, and an angelic smile. Her students adored her, and their parents well liked her.

The two couples had been gone for several hours when the phone call came from the hospital to the Hoard home. For whatever reason, the hospital did not relay the whole truth to the anxious parents, only that there had been an accident.

Unsure of Mae's condition, Kellis, Anna, and Zoe hastily left for St. Joseph Hospital, an hour away. Fourteen-year-old LeNore did not go but stayed home with Grandpa.

The family hurried with only the faintest light from the first quarter moon illuminating the now darkened sky. Each was familiar with the drive, but never had the ordinary journey seemed so slow or dark. Grandpa Long often said after yet another trip, "If we could only drag this farm 23 miles to the east." Never was that magic needed more than tonight.

Arriving at St. Joseph Hospital, the Emergency Room doctors told the Hoards their second-born daughter and sister died during transport to the hospital. About 8 p.m., the Ford had skidded on loose gravel and overturned on Covington Road and landed upside down in a three-foot ditch, about five miles west of Fort Wayne. The family learned Albert Bullerman, a Fort Wayne councilman, was nearby and put Mae in his car, where she died right before reaching St. Joe.[88] The doctors told the family Mae had died from a skull fracture. Information was initially scarce, and the family wouldn't learn all the details until reading multiple newspaper accounts from the scene later.

A flood of questions overwhelmed Mae's grieving parents and sister. Had Mae felt pain? What was the condition of the other three passengers? Did the car malfunction? Were they run off the road by another driver? Why was their beautiful daughter, who would have been 21 on Christmas Day, now lying dead in the morgue at St. Joe Hospital? None of it made any sense and wouldn't for a long time.

---

[88] "Indiana School Teacher Killed in Auto Accident." *The Star Press*. Muncie, Indiana, August 28, 1922.

Grandpa Long and LeNore sat vigil at the farm, not knowing if Mae was alive or dead. Washington must have pondered the loss of two beloved granddaughters. Calvin and Elizabeth Huffman Long lost a baby, Mary May Long, to enteritis, in 1904. Washington's 13-year-old granddaughter, Cleo Pearl Long, also a daughter of Calvin and Elizabeth Huffman Long, died of pneumonia in January 1914. A child's death—a grandchild's death—was outside of regular order. Cleo was often on Washington's mind. He also thought of his son Franklin, gone too soon.

In the wee hours, LeNore spotted the family car's distinctive round headlights in the driveway. A weary Kellis, Anna, and Zoe arrived home with dreadful news. Running outside into Kellis's arms, LeNore learned the terrible news Mae was dead.

Grandpa Long embraced Anna and Zoe.

Devastated, LeNore wandered into the front yard, staring at the sky. The sky, which had only the mournful first quarter moon earlier, was now lighted by a cornucopia of stars. Brighter than all the rest was the indigo blue Venus, the symbol of love.

LeNore would never forget the pain of that night. Her private brilliant celestial being, her beloved sister, was gone. With Mae's untimely death, a bright light sparkled and disappeared over the horizon.

LeNore would grieve forever. She would go out of her way to avoid Covington Road and did not like having to cross it as the primary route to Fort Wayne.

Mae's body was moved from the hospital by hearse to Miller and Pook Funeral Home in South Whitley in the early morning hours.

On Monday, both the morning and evening Fort Wayne newspapers featured the young teacher's death across the top of page one. *The Journal Gazette* used a "Second Coming" typeface, a font so large it had an apocalyptic name.

THE WEATHER
INDIANA—Fair, Monday and probably Tuesday; warmer Monday.

FORT WAYNE JOURNAL-GAZETTE

THE PEOPLE'S PAPER—FORT WAYNE AND NORTHERN INDIANA'S LEADING HOME NEWSPAPER AND WANT AD MEDIUM

12 PAGES TODAY

FOUNDED GAZETTE 1863   [NEWS OF THE WORLD]   MONDAY MORNING, AUGUST 28, 1922.   [BY THE ASSOCIATED PRESS]   PRICE THREE CENTS

GIRL KILLED IN HIGHWAY AUTO ACCIDENT

The newspapers noted Thomas McCoy and Mae were sitting in the back of the automobile, with Lawrence Schrader driving and Esther Moyer in the front. *The Journal Gazette* reported, "The tragedy occurred Sunday night about eight o'clock about five miles west of Fort Wayne and was the direct result of a broken steering apparatus. The road was wide and level at the point where the car left it and went over the grade, and there is abundant proof they were not going fast."[89]

The car turned "turtle" as it went off the road, and both Mae and Thomas McCoy were thrown clear of the vehicle. Pinned under the wreckage, both Schrader and Moyer got out quickly with only bruises.

The Hoard home bustled with visitors for days until the Washington Center Evangelical United Brethren Church funeral and Mae's burial at Eberhart Cemetery. The coroner's report, released a week after the accident, stated the steering apparatus had buckled under the driver and caused the accident.[90]

Mae's death hung like a storm cloud over the Hoard family, especially during the Christmas holidays, as Mae would have celebrated her 21st birthday on December 25.

∼

The following January, LeNore and her friend Ralph Wise skated with friends on Huffman Ditch, which fed into Sugar Creek. *The Garrett Clipper* reported on January 11, 1923, "the two had a narrow escape from an icy, muddy grave when the ice gave way beneath their feet, and they sank into three feet of water. The muddy bottom of the ditch gave way to their weight, and they became mired and were gradually sinking." The article explained the children's friends loudly captured Lemuel Bollinger's attention, who was chopping wood nearby. Bollinger rescued the children and took them to a nearby farmhouse. They were soon hurried home for warm clothing and recovery from the exposure.[91]

---

[89] "Girl Killed in Highway Auto Accident," *The Fort Wayne Journal-Gazette*, Fort Wayne, Indiana, August 28, 1922, Page 1 banner headline across width of page 1.
[90] "Logan Osman Dies Today, "*The Fort Wayne News-Sentinel*, August 28, 1922, pp. 1-3.
[91] No headline....It was learned from Columbia City on Tuesday that..., *The Garrett Clipper*, Garrett, Indiana, January 11, 1923.

Kellis and Anna could have easily lost a second daughter and perhaps her friend if Lemuel Bollinger weren't Johnny-on-the-spot. Mae's presence was always felt but rarely discussed. The loss left a massive hole in her parents' hearts and an unresolved cleft between the remaining sisters.

26 Not-So-Roaring Twenties

The Roaring Twenties are remembered for glamour, celebrity, gin mills, and the Charleston dance. Cities grew, business boomed, talkies came to theatres, and newspapers and magazines were full of lifestyle and culture trends. Hemlines came up, and inhibitions went down.

The high life of the Roaring Twenties bypassed the American farm family. Agricultural innovations brought record crop yields, yet low farm prices financially hamstrung farmers. Prices stayed down throughout the entire decade and into the 1930s. During World War I, the government had asked farmers to increase wartime crop growth. Excess crops led to reduced prices, and trouble for farmers. Ironically, farmers had become a victim of their success, and to an extent, their patriotism.

Kellis was developing a reputation for good corn and was noted by newspapers in two different years. *The Garrett Clipper,* on August 18, 1924, noted, "Kellis Hoard of Whitley County has one of the best fields of corn in this part of the state. It consists of 47 acres, and the stalks stand higher than a man's head well out in tassel and with large ears on it." The same newspaper gave Kellis a nod on July 21, 1927, "Kellis Hoard of near Columbia City has six acres of corn which he states is now shoulder-high and is commencing to tassel out. It is the most advanced corn in the county."

Despite the farm's excellent yields, the income didn't cover the bills. Mae had been a teacher, living at home. Had she contributed to the family income? Did her funeral expenses cause a financial problem? For the most part, Anna lived more frugally than she was raised. Albina favored shopping for Anna in Fort Wayne, but Anna eschewed furs and fancy feather hats for her daughters. Of course, styles had changed, but Anna and Zoe were handy with a sewing needle and made many of their clothes. The Hoards needed money and took out a $4,000 mortgage on their acreage in 1922.

Washington Long had no debt, kept his head above water, and still traveled to Florida every winter as a snowbird where he lived on Twigg Street in Tampa.

The crops grown on the Hoard and Long farms in the 1920s included corn, oats, wheat, and hay. As the horse population declined, so did the production of oats used primarily to feed them. In some areas of Whitley County, the soil was mucky, and farmers grew potatoes, onions, and mint. The Hoard and Long farms' soil was rich and suited for grain crops, leading to their high yields.[92]

LOGGING REMAINED A STEADY SOURCE OF INCOME FOR THE FARM. KELLIS HOARD IS SHOWN HAULING LOGS TO THE SOUTH WHITLEY MILL ON HIS 50TH BIRTHDAY, MARCH 1, 1920. FAMILY PHOTO.

---

[92] McVay, William G., History of the Long-Hoard-Enz-McVay Farm, Washington Township, Whitley County, Indiana. West Lafayette, Indiana, IN: Family History Booklet, 2010.

One source of income for the farm was selling eggs. The chickens were Anna's responsibility with help from her daughters who washed and crated the eggs in the home's cellar.

A 1929 grain elevator fire at the Farmers' Elevator in South Whitley destroyed many local farmers' uninsured wheat crop in storage. The Hoards were fortunate to have crop insurance, as many did not.

National farm income fell from a high of $16.9 billion in 1919 to only $5.3 billion in 1932.[93] What would later be called The Great Depression arrived early in the heartland, where families depended on income from seasonal crops. Many Whitley County farmers eventually lost their farms, and some men committed suicide over their seemingly unsolvable financial woes. Others lived hand-to-mouth, surviving on what they could grow. After the financial crash in 1929, the Great Depression came to the cities where troubled times meant great hunger. Most farm families grew vegetable gardens and raised hogs, chicken, and cattle. By canning foods, most were able to survive until the following year's crops came in. Farmers lived an austere life for nearly a decade before the stock market crash. The country needed national leadership. Who would provide it and when would it come?

---

[92] Walbert, David. "The Depression for Farmers." Link to NCpedia main page. North Carolina History Online Resource. Accessed March 18, 2021. https://www.ncpedia.org.

Amy McVay Abbott

27 The Klan with a K

Transportation in and out of Whitley County changed after the Great War. Passenger trains crisscrossed east and west, north, and south in the continental United States, with platformed stations in many small burgs like South Whitley. Citizens discovered new ease of travel. With new mobility, both whites and blacks from the southern states headed north for factory jobs.

For the first time since the American Revolution, urban cities out-populated rural areas. Agriculture had provided the most jobs since the country's founding; now, opportunities had increased in manufacturing jobs in the cities. Agriculture would never again have the economic heft it did in the previous century.

America's original sin of terrible treatment of blacks worsened in the twenties. Jim Crow laws resurfaced in the American south, and the Ku Klux Klan organized all over the country. Lynchings of people of color happened frequently. Jews and Catholics were harassed. White Hoosiers fell right in line, and many cities and towns became known as "sundown towns," areas that did not allow a black person to stay beyond sundown. Both Columbia City and South Whitley were sundown towns, staying "white on purpose."[94]

The Klan arrived in Whitley County in January 1923. *The Evening Post* featured an advertisement inviting the public to hear a speaker "compare the truth about the Klan with the stories you have heard from its enemies."[95] The speaker shared that one out of every five men in Indiana

---

[94] Loewen, James W. Sundown Towns: A Hidden Dimension of American Racism. New York (N.Y.): The New Press, 2018.
[95] Egner, Willadene. "Whitley County Survives the Ku Klux Klan." *Bulletin of the Whitley County Historical Society*, October 1986.

belonged to the Klan and also stated he knew 30 or 40 state legislators who were members.[96]

Few, if any, blacks lived in Whitley County, but for the next four years, Klansmen would meet in secret and parade in public, donned in their robes, in South Whitley, Churubusco, and Columbia City. Klansmen burned their share of fiery crosses at the homes of Catholics, Jews, and people who didn't support their efforts.

> They gave a parade in South Whitley, which attracted a large crowd along the street. A robed Klansman carrying an American flag led the parade. Behind him came six robed riders and horses and automobiles, decorated with crosses and flowers, followed by robed Klansmen.[97]

It is incomprehensible to believe anyone in Whitley County was unaware of the Klan's presence. In 1923, when LeNore was a freshman, many people heard the Reverend D.R. Moss of Fort Wayne at Washington Center High School. The crowd was so large that many had to listen from outside. Reverend Moss told the crowds, "The Klan stands for the supremacy of the white race."

Certain churches in Whitley County expressed vocal opposition and sometimes protested. Dunkard and Brethren congregations actively worked against the Klan.[98] Some Hoosiers considered Klan participation was similar to a church or social activity. In 1924, the following Card of Thanks appeared in a local newspaper,

> "As a family, we desire to express our thanks to all our neighbors and friends who were so good and kind to our son and brother and us during his sickness and death. We want to thank the Ku Klux Klan, the singers, and the Reverend X, also all for the beautiful flower offerings."[99]

---

[96] Egner, Willadene. "Whitley County Survives the Ku Klux Klan." *Bulletin of the Whitley County Historical Society*, October 1986.

[97] Egner, Willadene. "Whitley County Survives the Ku Klux Klan." *Bulletin of the Whitley County Historical Society*, October 1986.

[98] There is no record of any family members who belonged to the Klan. Most of the family attended the Dunkard or Brethren churches, who were vocally and actively opposed to the Klan.

[99] "Card of Thanks," *The Herald*, Huntington, Indiana, January 8, 1924. Names removed.

Indeed, it wasn't an ordinary social event like the Farm Bureau or the church youth league. The Indiana Klan committed crimes under cover of darkness with almost complete license. And yet, the Klan continued to march in local parades—sometimes unhooded—to the cheers of friends and family in Whitley County towns.

The Klan continued to grow in Whitley County, becoming Indiana Klan #25, eventually dying out within the decade.

By the end of the decade, the Klan had all but collapsed in Indiana. In 1930, however, a double lynching of two black men in Marion, about an hour south of Whitley County, was credited to the Klan's remnants.[100] As late as the 1970s, newspaper photographers in Madison County captured unmasked Klan members at Elwood and Anderson civic functions.

---

[100] Ksander, Yaël. "Ku Klux Klan." Moment of Indiana History - Indiana Public Media. Accessed March 18, 2021. https://indianapublicmedia.org/momentofindianahistory/ku-klux-klan/.

28 Pell Mell to the Devil

Zoe woke in her childhood bed, upstairs at the farm. How quiet it was. Next to where Zoe lay was an identical twin bed made up with Anna's "Grandmother's Flower Garden" yellow quilt. That was Mae's bed. Zoe and Mae had shared the big comfortable room upstairs. In a few days, it would be four years since Mae died in a car accident. Another upstairs bedroom was empty. Zoe's baby sister LeNore had started nurses' training at Lutheran Hospital in Fort Wayne.

Anna and Kellis appreciated Zoe living at home. Without LeNore's sizeable personality, the farm seemed like a different place. But only a trickle of sadness this morning because today was Old Settlers' Day. Today was a day to celebrate friends, neighbors, and recognize a shared history.

Anna woke her father, Washington, in the front bedroom the Hoards had added when he moved in. In the latter years of his life, Washington seemed aged and often forgetful. He moved in with his daughter and son-in-law in the new house down the hill from his own around 1919. Anna washed and ironed his clothes, as he set great store by how he looked, especially on a big day like today.

Kellis and the hired man managed the farming at both the Hoard farm and Washington's farm on the other side of Sugar Creek.

It was Thursday, August 19, 1926. Today might be a special day for Washington. He didn't know yet. Since 1909, Whitley County had awarded loving cups to the oldest registered settler and the longest continuous resident at Old Settlers' Days.

Would he be first in line to register at the Old Settlers' tent near the Courthouse? Would this be the year he won a silver cup?

135

Anna helped her father dress. He put on a lightweight summer suit and vest and added his gold watch, which hung on a chain. Despite the expected heat, he put on a tie.

OSD 1926 POSTCARD
COURTESY OF THE
PEABODY PUBLIC LIBRARY

Kellis got his Ford out of the barn and pulled the reliable machine in front of the farmhouse door. The early morning sky was cloud-free and as blue as the perennial periwinkles that overgrew on the south side of the summer kitchen—a perfect day for a festival. Zoe, Anna, and Washington got in the car, and they were off, east on the Washington Center Road past the school where LeNore had graduated in May. They headed north on Indiana State Road 11 (later Indiana State Road 9) to the Whitley County Courthouse.

The stately courthouse in the middle of town was the center of Old Settlers' Day events. The French Renaissance-style building rose to three stories of Indiana limestone, topped with an iron-covered dome. A few people wandered inside to see the relics room, treasures belonging to the first white settlers of Whitley County.

Registration began at 9 a.m. The South Whitley and Columbia City high school bands played lively music for those waiting in line.

The day featured events for the whole family, a greased pole climbing contest, free children's show at the Columbia Theatre, and a horseshoe pitching contest with cash prizes at the Gun Club.

For Washington, the highlight was the official, early afternoon Old Settlers' Day ceremony in front of the courthouse. Ralph Gates, a local attorney, and future governor of Indiana, gave a welcome, followed by the Reverend Charles Watkins of Muncie, who gave a lengthy speech entitled, "Faith of our Fathers."

Reverend Watkins, a Baptist, urged the large crowd to remember that the first structure in pioneer life was the home, followed by the church, followed by the school. "It is just a short distance to a church nowadays

Programme
26TH ANNUAL WHITLEY COUNTY
OLD SETTLERS DAY

COLUMBIA CITY, INDIANA
THURSDAY, AUG. 19, '26

9:00 A. M.—Registration of old settlers in court house
Opening of relic room by J. H. Shilts
Concert by South Whitley and Columbia City School Bands under direction of Prof. Phil Farren
Horseshoe pitching contest at Gun Club grounds; Cash Prizes
Gun Club Shoot at club grounds; Cash Prizes

10:00 A. M.—Children's Free Show at Columbia Theatre
Climbing of greased pole; Cash Prizes
Songs by Chief White Wing
Free act by James B. Hawk, champion rope thrower

11 to 12 A. M.—Music and Free Acts

1:00 P. M.—Concert by South Whitley and Columbia City Bands
Solos by Miss Irene Worden

1:45 P. M.—Address of Welcome from band stand by Hon. R. F. Gates
Address, "The Faith of Our Fathers"—Hon. Charles Watkins, Muncie, Ind.
Presentation of cups by Rev. L. A. Luckenbill
Report of historian—R. H. Maring
Report of nominating committee
Solos—Miss Irene Worden
Setting off of flagshells from aeroplane

3:00 P. M.—Concert by Dixie Harmony Boys, featuring Julia Janoski and Harry Nutter, vocalists
Gun Club Shoot and Horseshoe pitching continued until 4 p. m.
Base Ball—Fort Wayne Colored Giants vs Columbia City Modern Woodmen at Carter Field

3:30 P. M.—Hog Calling Contest from band stand; Cash Prizes

4:30 P. M.—Grace Gage, contortionist and her Two Trained Dogs

5:00 P. M.—Songs by Chief White Wing
Free act by James B. Hawk, champion rope thrower

7:00 P. M.—Concert by Dixie Harmony Boys
Musical Free Act

8:00 P. M.—Concert by South Whitley and Columbia City School Bands
Free Act by Grace Gage, contortionist and Trained Dogs

9:00 P. M.—An illuminated aeroplane will set off glorious fireworks and a 25 minute display will be terminated the setting off of a milli....

OSD 1926 PROGRAMME
COURTESY OF THE PEABODY PUBLIC LIBRARY

by machine. The importance of religion cannot be overestimated," said Reverend Watkins.[101]

"How much faith have the people in the future generation of boys and girls today?" the speaker asked.[102]

Washington was widely known to enjoy liberal religious views and supported several religious organizations financially. He may have thoroughly enjoyed the zeal of the speaker. Or his attention might have wandered to the Civil War monument on the courthouse lawn which honored the Whitley County Civil War dead.

Reverend Watkins answered his question about the future generation of boys and girls. "I do not feel the flapper, or the drug store sheik would fall when they came to meet their duties and responsibilities of life. One evidence of age frequently manifested was to begin to criticize the younger generation because they do not do like the other person did when he was a boy and to think that they are going pell-mell to the devil."[103]

The sun was still high above on this early August afternoon. Some elders nodded off during the featured address, lunch and the hot sun bringing on a nap.

The Post noted Watkins concluded his remarks by saying the boys and girls who make love in automobiles are no different than their parents who used to tie their reins around the whip and let Old Dobbin find his way home.[104]

Finally, the Reverend L.A. Luckenbill rose to present the two loving cups, one for the oldest resident and one for the most senior continuous resident.

"The winner of the oldest resident is Isaiah Johnson of Thorncreek Township," said Reverend Luckenbill. "Mr. Johnson was born on December 10, 1835, and is now 90 years, five months, and nine days."

---

[101] "The Aftermath of the Annual Old Settlers' Day." *The Post*, Columbia City, Indiana, August 20, 1926.
[102] "The Aftermath of the Annual Old Settlers' Day." *The Post*, Columbia City, Indiana, August 20, 1926.
[103] "The Aftermath of the Annual Old Settlers' Day." *The Post*, Columbia City, Indiana, August 20, 1926.
[104] Old Settlers' Day program, Columbia City, Indiana, Thursday, August 19, 1926, records of the Peabody Library, Columbia City, Indiana.

So much for being the most senior resident. The family held its collective breath. How many others here today had been born in a log cabin in Whitley County? In 1845?

"The longest continuous resident for 1926 is Washington Long of Washington Township. Mr. Long was born in Washington Township on February 23, 1845, and is 81 years, five months, and 27 days."[105]

Washington walked proudly to the bandstand, his green registration tag attached to his jacket lapel, his gold watch chain glimmering in the afternoon sun. He surveyed the large crowd that had gathered all along Van Buren from Main to Chauncey Street.

Reverend Luckenbill asked him to elucidate on his award.

"Things ain't like they used to was," said the 81-year resident of Whitley County. And then he went back to his chair and sat to thunderous applause. Washington's statement on constant change has become a family saying for generations.

The Hoards enjoyed visiting with friends into the evening as Washington accepted congratulations from friends and family.

The Fort Wayne Colored Giants played the Columbia City Modern Woodmen at Carter Field in baseball. Others attended the Hog Calling Contest at the Band Stand, which offered cash prizes for the best call. For people who missed her afternoon show, Grace Gage,

OLD SETTLERS' DAY LOVING CUP
1926 LONGEST RESIDENT OF WHITLEY COUNTY,
AWARDED TO WASHINGTON LONG.
PHOTO BY RANDY ABBOTT.

[105] "The Aftermath of the Annual Old Settlers' Day." *The Post*, Columbia City, Indiana, August 20, 1926.

contortionist, and her two trained dogs gave a special performance on the courthouse lawn. Darkness came, and an illuminated aeroplane flew low above the crowd, followed by a 25-minute display of firework shells over Columbia City.

After a special day, the family returned home, still delighted Washington had finally received his due as a pioneer. He would not compete again, believing others should have their chance. His loving cup, however, became a treasured family heirloom.

29 A Death and A Birth

As a second-year nursing student, LeNore Hoard observed a Caesarean-section delivery in the Lutheran Hospital's surgery suite. How did she grab the plum assignment, scrubbing in with the hospital's leading

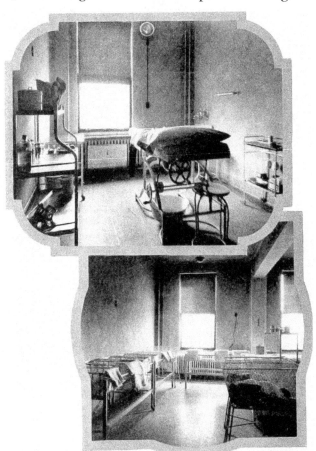

DELIVERY ROOM AND NURSERY,
LUTHERAN HOSPITAL.
IMAGE SOURCE:
SCHOOL OF NURSING YEARBOOK, 1929

Top: Delivery Room. Bottom: Nursery.

obstetrician? The delivery room, part of the more extensive surgical suite, wasn't more than 15-feet square. With medical equipment, the surgeon, and all his assistants, the place felt crowded.

The patient, anesthetized with morphine and scopolamine, delivered a female infant with auburn hair like her own. Like most C-section babies, she was plump and pink. Everyone appeared to be okay, mother and child.

The doctor handed the baby to the young nurse. LeNore cleaned her of amniotic fluid and blood, weighed her, and checked her respirations. Nine pounds, three ounces. A big baby, indeed. The student nurse wrapped the baby in a warm blanket. Following the doctor's instructions, she took the infant girl to the waiting room to meet her father. LeNore left the operating room with the baby. The doctor removed the placenta and surveyed the instruments on a tray, ready to stitch the patient's wound.

LeNore walked the long, white-tiled hallway with the newborn baby cradled in her arms. The second-year student nurse saw the new father on the other side of the surgical suite's large double doors through the porthole-style windows. She used her back to open the door carefully, holding the bundled infant closely.

In the waiting room, Carl August Enz paced back and forth. His wife, Alma Mahler Enz was admitted hours ago with severe pains. He wasn't allowed in the labor room, a narrow, dark room with multiple patients in varying stages of labor. The doctor had talked with Carl around noon to let him know Alma would have a C-section.

The baby appears to be large, the doctor told Carl. We want to get him or her out of there.

That had been nearly two hours ago.

The double doors swung open and a nurse, covered in surgical garb from head-to-toe like an ancient white sovereign, approached him with the baby in her arms. He couldn't see the nurse's entire face, though her blue eyes looked directly into his.

"Meet your daughter, Mr. Enz," said LeNore, handing him the bundle.

Carl sat and took the baby from LeNore.

"She is so beautiful," he said to no one in particular, and then to his baby, "You are so beautiful."

LeNore gave Carl a few minutes with his daughter and then said, "I need to take her back to the nursery. Your wife's doctor will be out soon with an update."

But the doctor didn't come right away.

When LeNore carried the newborn back into the surgical area, she overheard the loud whispers of her fellow nurses. Something in their tone alarmed her. Uneasy, after taking the baby to the nursery, she returned to her observation post in the surgical suite.

On the delivery table, Alma was bleeding profusely. While the doctor tried to close the surgical site, the patient began to hemorrhage and bleed out.

Alma's blood pressure lowered precipitously, and her heart rate slowed. The small room was now crowded with additional medical personnel who had not been there only ten minutes earlier when LeNore left with the baby.

Still semi-conscious from the anesthesia, Alma lost blood faster than the nurses could clean. LeNore pressed her back tightly against the wall to allow the hospital's chaplain to pass.

Did Alma even know she had delivered a beautiful baby girl?

The doctors tried heroic measures. Shortly after four p.m., Alma's heart gave out as her blood pressure dropped too low to sustain her life. LeNore looked at the big white clock on the wall, as did the doctor.

"Time of death, 4:04 p.m., September 21, 1928, Year of Our Lord," said the doctor, as he took off his glasses and motioned for another nurse to wipe his brow. He mumbled again under his surgical mask, "Year of Our Lord."

The patient lay motionless on the delivery room table, the chaplain remaining at her head. The nursing supervisor gingerly pulled a sheet over the dead patient's body, slowly as if she might still injure her.

The doctor left the operating room; he had other patients in labor. For a minute, the remaining staff stood over Alma's body. The death hit them hard. Although each staff member knew his or her role, they stood immobilized by losing this lovely young woman. Maternity deaths had become rarer since the turn of the century, especially in hospital births. Why this woman? Why today? The late afternoon sun cast an indifferent light through the windows at the back of the room.

Within a minute or two, the staff started to clean the room and prepare for the next patient.

As LeNore left the day shift, Alma's physician delivered the most horrific news to the new father in the waiting room.

LeNore and her fellow student nurses donned their blue and red wool Lutheran Hospital nursing capes to leave for student housing. A recent shift arrived—caring for patients giving birth, others having elective surgery, still others dying of old age. Hospitals, like life, had an ebb and flow that persisted no matter what. The hospital reverberated with shift change activity as LeNore left, the rhythm of hospital life continued, impervious to the great joy or pain within.

LeNore walked along the sidewalk through the grove of white birch trees whose leaves were turning an autumn color. The leaves would be golden and shimmer like Colorado aspens before falling to the cold ground in another month. She thought about the young mother, a year or two older than herself. She wondered if the young first-time father could care for his baby. She wondered if the baby would be placed in an orphanage.

In the oncoming chill of the autumn evening, LeNore pulled her blue and red wool cape around her and ran home, dismissing her thoughts about the man and his baby.

30 Zoe's Near Miss

Zoe loved having an automobile. She had taught at district schools for several years and saved money to buy her vehicle. Zoe and her friend, Louise Johnson, also a schoolteacher, drove to Columbia City for shopping and visits with friends. Summer was around the corner, the school year had ended, and being young and free and owning a new car was glorious. Zoe and Louise celebrated with a trip to town. The young women wanted the latest fabric to make lightweight summer dresses.[106]

Zoe parked her machine, and the young women went into Flox's Department Store.

Within a minute, the teachers and the store employees heard a commotion and gun shots outside the store. Zoe and Louise witnessed the shooting and soon followed the Flox employees to the store's backroom for safety.

Three bandits had gone into the Columbia State Bank next door, waving Tommy guns. Men with machine guns robbed the bank, while the getaway driver stayed in the car.

Inside the bank, the robbers forced an employee at gunpoint to open the vault which contained $50,000, securities, and other essential documents. The employee fumbled with the vault combination. Two of the bandits pulled out an open cash drawer and ransacked a thousand dollars. Pulling out the drawer rang a silent bell to the police station.

As police approached, one of the gang members shot out into the street. He killed Mrs. Fred Binder, 40, who had been watching the action from her second-story apartment across the street. The bandit also shot Mrs.

---

[106] *The Garrett Clipper,* Garrett, Indiana, Monday, April 22, 1929, page 6.

145

Eva Harshbarger, 40, who happened to be on the sidewalk in front of the bank.

Sheriff J.M. Haynes was shot in the shoulder and taken to the hospital, along with Mrs. Harshbarger. Neither had critical injuries, but the bandits escaped and left Columbia City. An eyewitness saw one of the gang stagger out of the bank and fall. The robber was carried to the getaway car by his companions. Another robber was drenched in blood. In the chaos, the four bank robbers drove away, heading west on State Road 30.

As soon as the robbery had begun, it was over. Zoe and Louise came out from the backroom to find police cars and officers and city officials around the bank site. Zoe's car sported bullet holes in the headlamp, the windshield, and the car top. A reporter asked Zoe and Louise their feelings about the frightening event. The women replied, "It was the most horrible thing we've ever seen."[107]

On the following Sunday, crowds came to Columbia City to view the crime scene. The bank windows were splattered with blood and broken. Strauss Brothers Clothing Store, on the other side of the bank, had large bullet holes in each of its three plate-glass windows.

An area newspaper reported, "Thousands of persons crowded this city yesterday to see the bullet-marked bank front and other damage done by the flying lead let loose by Sheriff Haynes, his deputies, and the desperadoes who fought their way out of a trap."[108]

The Columbia State Bank robbery was the eleventh robbery in Indiana since New Year's Day 1929 and was a harbinger of crimes to come. Hoosier John Dillinger, "Public Enemy Number One," filled the newspapers with his crimes until the FBI shot him outside a Chicago theatre in 1934.[109]

---

[107] *The Garrett Clipper,* Garrett, Indiana, Monday, April 22, 1929, page 6, story didn't indicate which woman was quoted.
[108] *The Garrett Clipper,* Garrett, Indiana, Monday, April 22, 1929, page 6.
[109] https://www.history.com/topics/crime/john-dillinger.

31 The Second Chance Encounter

In white uniforms and crisp nurse caps, three long rows of new nurses posed for the photographer in front of the Lutheran Hospital. Graduation day, August 29, 1929, was the day to celebrate the end of backbreaking double shifts and sweaty surgical suits. The young women said goodbye to late-night cramming for pharmacology tests and the end of lost holidays and weekends with their families. These young nurses stepped up on the lower rung of the professional staff ladder, higher

LeNore Hoard's Nursing Class. Family photo.

than the nurses in school. This was the day the student nurses had been waiting for since August 1926.

Kellis, Anna, Zoe, and Grandpa Long sat in folding chairs and watched LeNore receive her diploma. Earlier that morning, the nurses received their nurse's pins, a tradition dating back to Queen Victoria who recognized Florence Nightingale's heroism in the Crimean War. Nursing programs adopted the custom of pinning recent graduates.

August 1929 was an essential and bittersweet time for Kellis and Anna Hoard. In the early part of the month, they watched LeNore celebrate the completion of her diploma. Zoe was soon moving to South Bend to take a job at Battell School. Now free of the training schedule, LeNore visited the farm about once a month, as did Zoe, usually on the same weekend.

LeNore passed the Indiana State nursing boards and received her first Indiana State Nursing License on September 9. She accepted a nursing position in the Well-Baby Clinic at Lutheran Hospital. What a relief for the young nurse to get a job in a challenging economy!

Most Friday and Saturday evenings, LeNore and her friends went out. The young women copied the clothing styles from *Harper's Bazaar* and *Vogue*, sleek, colorful, at-the-knee dresses that sometimes caused a raised eyebrow in LeNore's rural home community.

IMAGE COURTESY OF EMBASSY THEATER.

LeNore and Zoe both wore their brunette hair bobbed like Fort Wayne's film star Carole Lombard. Both sisters were tall and lean. LeNore had an oval face with straight jet-black hair and perfect skin; Zoe had dark curly hair, was tall and slim, and had a winning smile and a less dramatic personality. Both were whip-smart; Zoe more ambitious, LeNore more flirtatious.

LeNore, her roommates, and often Zoe watched Hollywood films at the downtown Fort Wayne theaters. The young women took the Calhoun Street trolley downtown for ten cents and caught Saturday matinees if they didn't have a date. Or their dates drove them in brightly-colored soft-top roadsters to see the latest film at the Majestic or the Emboyd.

LeNore had a steady boyfriend, an Indiana University law student, but she was in Fort Wayne. Porter, her beau, was in Bloomington, and LeNore liked to flirt. Absence, in this case, did not make her heart grow fonder for her steady fellow. Before they broke up, Porter gave LeNore a gorgeous set of cultured pearls, still owned by a family member nearly a century later.

LeNore's roommates were sometimes upset with her flirtatiousness toward their gentlemen callers. LeNore intrigued the young men who came to Kinnaird Avenue to pick up their dates. As she would for the rest of her life, LeNore could put on a charm offensive which the men found attractive and amusing, but her roommates, not so much. With her sleek looks, blue eyes, and winsome figure, LeNore rarely found her dance card blank.

Despite the social whirl of the weekends, on Mondays, the young nurse was in her stiff cap and white, perfectly pressed uniform, ready to report to the clinic before 8 a.m.

One fall afternoon, LeNore's co-workers chattered because a man sat in the waiting room with a child. Fathers were out of place in the clinic, generally packed with mothers and babies who needed attention for pertussis and diphtheria shots or usual complaints. Fathers worked or looked for work. Fathers did not bring children to the clinic, especially a man as impeccably tailored as this one. He was tall and lean, with dark hair combed perfectly to fit his

CARL ENZ, HOLDING HIS INFANT DAUGHTER, DONNA.
FAMILY PHOTO.

oval face. He wore a well-made suit and wingtips so shiny they reflected the overhead lights. He held an infant who looked female and about a year old on his lap. The child didn't look much like him and had a rosy, pink complexion and beautiful auburn hair.

From behind the reception counter, LeNore had a good look at him. She noticed how tall he was, and oh, my, that full head of jet-black hair. Something about him was familiar, but LeNore couldn't place him. She flipped through the charts before her, "Dettmer, Enz, Knake, Kunburger, Zollinger." Was the name Enz familiar?

LeNore asked a co-worker if she recognized the man. Yes, the co-worker said, that's the man whose wife died in childbirth last fall. Don't you remember how sad it was? The nursing supervisor heard the young nurses' discussion and chastised them quietly for talking about a patient.

"Ladies, stop daydreaming and take this patient back," instructed the nursing supervisor. She handed LeNore a file labeled "Donna Enz."

LeNore called out the name "Donna Enz." The man with the baby approached her with a big smile and laughing dark eyes.

"Don't I know you from somewhere?" he said.

32 The Death of Washington Long

In the latter years of his life, Washington Long made his home with his daughter Anna and her family. After the 1918 fire in the Hoard home, Kellis and Anna built a new Cape Cod-style home. Albina Long had passed away in 1917. Washington was lonely in his home on the hill near Sugar Creek. He moved in with his daughter and son-in-law in 1919. About the same time, he stopped active farming, and Kellis took over Washington's farm management. Washington kept his membership in the local farm and civic organizations and his church.

Wanting to avoid the confusion caused by his father dying without a will, Washington hired local attorney David V. Whiteleather[110] to write his will. The document featured all the usual legal jargon, plus this addition:

> "Item Two. I will, device, and bequeath to the Eberhard Cemetery Trustees and their successors in office One Hundred Dollars ($100). Said sum is to be held by said association and the income therefrom to be used for the upkeep and beautifying of my burial lot. No part of the principal shall be used for any purpose except to be loaned in which the income shall be received to carry out the above bequest."[111]

The will gave Calvin and Anna each half the acreage for their lifetimes through a legal method known as a life estate. Upon the passing of Washington's children, the acreage would pass to his grandchildren, Berniece and Beryl Long, Zoe and LeNore Hoard. A life estate could be

---

[110] John Whiteleather, Jr., David's grandson, served the family as attorney when the farm was sold in December 2010.
[111] Last Will and Testament of Washington Long, September 9, 1922, family document.

broken but required expensive legal wrangling and approval of all parties.

Washington remained active until about a year before his September 1, 1930 death. A stroke left him partially paralyzed, but he could still get around the house and occasionally go to town, church, or community events. Local newspapers sang his praises upon his death.

"Mr. Long was a Democrat in politics. He was a devout member of the United Brethren Church at Washington Center being consistently liberal in its financial support.

"The deceased was always interested in agriculture and the raising of livestock on his responsibility and was rewarded with encouraging success."[112]

Washington's funeral service was held at Eberhard Lutheran Church. His four remaining grandchildren, Berniece, Beryl, Zoe, and LeNore, acted as flower bearers. He was buried next to Albina in the Eberhard Cemetery under the red marble tombstone off Keiser Road.

The legacy farm had belonged to Washington because of his siblings' generosity in 1873 and the early passing of two brothers. Brother Lewis Long's shocking death in the Civil War followed Washington's father's passing in 1861. After their mother's death, the siblings gave their part of the legacy farm to Washington and Eliga, who had farmed the land since their father died. Eliga died in 1873, and the land passed solely to Washington.

He loved the land from his childhood until his 1930 death, despite his circuitous route to ownership. Upon his death, he was 85 years old, and except for his winter travels, he had lived in the same area all of his life.

---

[112] "Death Claims a Long and Useful Life." *Columbia City Post*, Columbia City, Indiana, September 2, 1930.

33 Late to The Wedding

Carl and LeNore began dating in late 1929. LeNore worked for Lutheran Hospital and took jobs as an in-home nurse for tuberculosis patients in northeast Indiana and northwestern Ohio.

Carl was an agricultural field man, traveling throughout Indiana, Illinois, and Ohio selling farm properties and managing company-owned land. The lovers weren't often in the same place and developed a nearly daily correspondence.

Only his letters remain, and tell their love story in Carl's own words. It's the account of a lonely man on the road, jealous of LeNore's active social schedule, and ready for a settled life.[113]

৵

Vases of red roses and red tulips filled the living room at the farm. Zoe hosted an engagement shower for LeNore on Valentine's Day 1931. Forty friends and relatives crowded into the front room to learn of and celebrate LeNore's upcoming April 12th wedding to Carl Enz. At each place setting sat a tiny red paper heart, which included heart-shaped pictures of the bride and groom and a dainty, cut-out Cupid with his arrow.

---

[113] Abbott, Amy McVay. Always Carl: Letters from the Heart and Heartland, 1929-1931. Newburgh, IN: 2019.

Carl was 30, and LeNore was 22. Their courtship was sporadic. Both had traveling jobs. She might have a three-week case in Ohio, while he might be on a long trip to southern Illinois. Somehow they managed to see each other and became serious in 1931. Carl purchased a home on Fairfax Avenue near Lutheran Hospital for himself, LeNore, and Donna and gave LeNore carte blanche and encouragement to decorate it however she pleased. He sold the home in which he and his first wife, Alma, had lived. Alma died the day their daughter, Donna, was born.

On the wedding morning, the Hoard farm's peach and plum trees bloomed fully, turning the orchard into a spring snowbank. The Hoard

and Enz families and two-year-old Donna met for lunch at the Hoard farm before the late afternoon ceremony in Fort Wayne.

At four p.m., the guests and attendants waited in St. Paul Lutheran Church's sanctuary. The bride and groom, along with the groom's daughter, had not yet arrived. The couple was late for their wedding, causing a last-minute commotion. A few minutes after the hour, they arrived. In their haste and confusion, Carl and LeNore seated little Donna in a pew by herself despite the presence of multiple grandparents who could step in to help.

CARL ENZ AND LENORE HOARD WEDDING PARTY. SEATED, GROOM CARL ENZ SEATED, BRIDE LENORE HOARD ON HIS RIGHT, MAID OF HONOR ZOE HOARD ON HIS LEFT, BEST MAN WALTER ENZ STANDING. FAMILY PHOTO.

LeNore was disorganized and unfocused and

generally late to any occasion, usually making a grand entrance. Carl, who also moved on his own time, may have stopped to chat with a farmer he saw outside. Who knows what happened? But what a grand entrance the bride made on her father's arm.

> "The bride appeared in a charming frock of peach taffeta fashioned with cream silk lace. She wore crystal beads, a large picture hat of tan mohair braid, and blond footwear. She carried an arm bouquet of talisman roses and a white prayer book the gift of her sister who attended her as maid of honor."[114]

Carl and LeNore made a handsome couple. Carl's brother Walter Enz served as the best man, with LeNore's sister Zoe as the maid of honor.

Within a few months of their wedding, Carl accepted a promotion with the Prudential Insurance Company in Springfield, Illinois. This job would have him on the road less.

On March 28, 1932, Marilyn Anne Enz was born at a Springfield hospital. Having lost his first wife in childbirth, Carl was beside himself with worry and decided he and LeNore would have no other children.

Grandma and Grandpa Hoard and Grandma Tillie Mahler (Donna's grandmother, Alma Mahler's mother) visited Springfield. Marilyn was baptized at the Hoard home over the summer by Reverend Paul Miller,

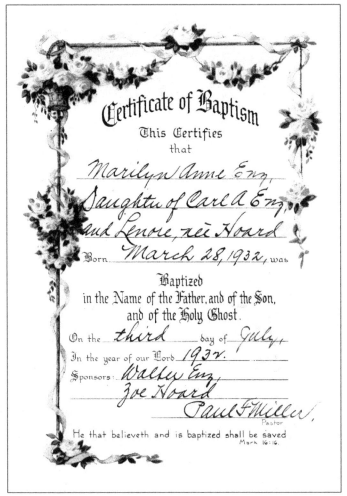

Certificate of Baptism

This Certifies
that

Marilyn Anne Enz,

Daughter of Carl A Enz,

and Lenore, née Hoard

Born *March 28, 1932,* was

Baptized
in the Name of the Father, and of the Son, and of the Holy Ghost.

On the *third* day of *July,*
In the year of our Lord *1932.*
Sponsors: *Walter Enz,*
Zoe Hoard
Paul F Miller,
Pastor

He that believeth and is baptized shall be saved
Mark 16:16.

---

114 "Nuptials Marked with Simplicity and Loveliness." *South Whitley Tribune*, South Whitley, Indiana, April 13, 1931.

the same pastor who married Carl and LeNore at St. Paul Lutheran Church. Zoe Hoard and Walter Enz served as Marilyn's godparents.

Carl rose in status within the company, receiving several promotions and winning sales awards. The family moved to a larger home in 1934, and it had a maid's quarter, so LeNore had help within the home. In the middle of the Great Depression, many middle-class people had help in their homes because it was inexpensive. Young, unmarried women found working for a family a great option that provided a salary, room, and bath. Working as a maid meant safety compared to other young, poor women in a state capitol with lonely male legislators and lobbyists looking for company.

LeNore belonged to many social clubs and enjoyed being the wife of a

rising businessman. Their new home, two-story and all-brick in an upscale neighborhood, had every amenity available in a city, including electricity. Both Carl and LeNore were used to living with electricity. Having electric power meant LeNore had an electric washer, a coffee maker, and a radio.

Many rural communities had yet to get power. At the farm, Anna still used kerosene lamps for light. She and Kellis had a radio for many years, but it depended on large batteries, which were not always available.

During summer vacations and holidays, the Enz family visited the farm and Carl's family in Fort Wayne. Donna loved the farm, and even little Marilyn enjoyed seeing the animals, walking the lane, and being with her grandparents. Kellis and Anna were both warm, the kind of people who ran out of the house to greet family when they arrived.

"I have a surprise for you," Kellis told Donna as he took her to help with chores in the white barn. Donna was about three or four. Kellis opened a little wooden box attached to the barn wall and pulled out two apples, which he peeled with his pocketknife. "I thought nothing could be better than this, sharing an apple with my grandfather on a nice summer day."[115]

Visits to the Enz grandparents in the Lakeside Park neighborhood of Fort Wayne stood in stark contrast to the Hoard farm with its garden, woods, animals, and endless adventures for a child. The Enz house was filled with uncomfortable, stiff furniture and Victorian-era wallpaper. Except for walks to the Lakeside Park Rose Garden, there was little for the granddaughters to do.

Then came Kellis's horrific and unexpected death, like a lightning bolt out of a clear sky. No one had considered he might pass at such a young age. What would become of the farm? Neither Zoe nor LeNore had the physical ability to work the farm, and it was questionable if they could take on the financial management. Both women were bright, and educated, but neither lived nearby nor had the inclination.

LeNore was happily married to a successful businessman, and Zoe had become an elementary school principal. The conundrum was complicated by a mortgage on Kellis and Anna's farm. Anna's father, Washington Long, had left the farm to his children, Calvin, and Anna, in a life estate. This meant neither Anna nor Calvin owned the land, however, they received its income during their lifetimes. Upon Anna's death, her parcel passed to Zoe and LeNore. Calvin's portion passed to his children, Beryl and Berniece. Anna could not sell the land without many legal expenses and permission by all affected parties. She had no idea what to do.

---

[115] Telephone conversation, Donna Enz Argon and author, April 10, 2016.

Amy McVay Abbott

34 Closing the Circle

Carl and LeNore and the girls stayed at the farm after Kellis's funeral. The sounds of small children brightened the entire house. Anna loved having her granddaughters close.

Anna was left alone on the farm, with an insufficient income to pay their mortgage and usual expenses. Farmers had been suffering from low crop prices for more than a decade.

She had a hired man, but he couldn't step in to manage the farm. Her situation jeopardized continued family ownership of the farm. Because the legacy farm was in life estate after Washington's death, Calvin and Anna received the income and were responsible for expenses but couldn't sell it. Breaking the will required legal wrangling and significant expense.

Many Whitley County farmers had already sold their farms or were forced into bankruptcy in the late 1920s and early 1930s. Now the entire country was in the Great Depression, and the economic outlook was bleak.

Early in 1933, President Franklin Roosevelt's first act was to increase farm prices. Much to Anna's surprise, help for her financial crisis would come from two different sources—a controversial policy of an untested President and her daughter's new husband and father-in-law.

Carl asked if he could speak to his mother-in-law alone. He told Anna he and LeNore, with the help of his father, Charles Enz, wanted to buy out Zoe and Anna's portion of the legacy farm as well as Kellis and Anna's 40 acres. If all the beneficiaries agreed—Anna, Zoe, and LeNore—Washington's will could be broken, and the legacy farm sold to Carl and LeNore. Washington's will specified different sections for Anna and Calvin, so Calvin did not need to approve the sale. Carl asked for her to think it over and asked for a meeting with Anna, Zoe, Charles, and LeNore.

Charles Enz became the hero of Anna's story. Charles ran his own land management business in Fort Wayne. Charles was amassing large amounts of farmland in both northwestern Ohio and northeastern Indiana. As a younger man, Charles managed ranches with thousands of acres for cattle-feeding in Ohio and Indiana.

Carl and Charles presented a stack of papers as the five sat around Anna's mahogany Duncan Phyfe table in the dining room. Outside the sizeable north-facing window lay the fields and the big white barn, the fencerows built by Kellis, and beyond, Sugar Creek.

Anna glanced out the window. Her memories of this land, all she had loved and lost, were bound in her mind like precious love letters in a ribbon. Her grandfather, Reuben, spent most of his life building the farm business. Washington had improved it, and Kellis had farmed both his and his father-in-law's adjacent acreage. For Anna, this rich Indiana land was a beloved place, every wildflower, every corn stalk, every fruit tree, even the gravel lane that ran back to the woods.

Carl explained he and LeNore wanted to buy out Zoe and Anna's portions of the land. But it was complicated, and all the legal action might take time.

Anna needed money to pay the mortgage and keep the farm going. She also needed a steady farm manager. Anna was still in relatively good health and enjoyed her regular chores, but could not manage the planting and harvesting, the larger animals, and the equipment. She typically had not managed the business transactions, buying, and selling grain, filing the taxes, managing the ditches and tiles, and repairing equipment.

Carl explained his father had offered to back Carl and LeNore in purchasing the farms. While the young couple had some of the cash needed, Charles would help with the remainder, using LeNore's portion as collateral.

An actuary would determine how the life estate would be split. Anna, who held the life estate, would get a portion of the proceeds, as would Zoe. All the proceeds from the 40 acres she owned with Kellis went to Anna. What Anna earned from the sale would sustain her for her life.

Anna agreed to the idea. Carl and LeNore went into debt to his father, and Anna repaid the 1922 mortgage that weighed her down. Her money and management worries disappeared. Carl and Charles took over the farm management.

Anna lived in the house for the rest of her life. Zoe and LeNore visited in the summers and on school vacations. Anna could revel worry-free in the summers she enjoyed so much, with her daughters and granddaughters visiting.

THIS AERIAL PHOTOGRAPH OF HOMELAND FARM WAS TAKEN IN 1947. THE FARM WAS LOVED AND CARED FOR BY FIVE GENERATIONS OF THE FAMILY AND SOLD IN 2010 AFTER 173 YEARS OF CONTINUOUS OWNERSHIP. FAMILY PHOTO.

LeNore and Carl returned to Springfield, where Carl continued advancement with Prudential. The couple frequently made the long trip between Springfield and Tunker, and LeNore took the girls and stayed at the farm most summers.

While driving the 300 miles between Springfield and Tunker, Carl and LeNore heard the sirens before seeing them. Looking back, LeNore told Carl they were being chased by multiple state police cars. Though LeNore could be melodramatic, Carl saw them and quickly pulled over. Several state police officers ran from their cars to the driver's side where Carl was waiting.

The policeman started to say something, and then he looked over at LeNore, who looked more curious than frightened. The man in blue followed LeNore's pointed finger to the backseat, where he saw a small girl and an infant sitting.

Carl's Buick was the same color and resembled John Dillinger's 1933 Terrapin. While there is no record of Dillinger owning a Buick, the family of four was stopped multiple times in areas where Dillinger had been.

That the driver immediately pulled over, had a wife in the passenger seat, and two small children in the back may have discouraged the police from pulling out their firearms.

The legal transfer of land from Anna to Carl and LeNore officially happened nearly a year later, on October 26, 1933.

APRIL 26, 1936,
ZOE HOARD MARRIES A. EVERITT EVANS AT HOMELAND FARM. FAMILY PHOTO.

The Enzes made some improvements to the property, including an upgrade of the home's bathroom. Carl removed the privy next to the house. He planted a plum tree where the outhouse stood, that grew to twice the size of the other plum trees in the garden. "Daddy would grin and say, it was special; it got good fertilizer," remembered Donna Enz Argon, about her father Carl Enz.[116]

Zoe returned to her school principal job in northern Indiana, where she met A. Everett Evans. She had moved to South Bend in 1929, taught two years at Battell School, and then served five years as principal of Twin Branch. She married A. Everett Evans at Anna's home on April 26, 1936, and resided in LaPorte, Indiana.

---

[116] Telephone conversation with Donna Enz Argon and author, April 10, 2016.

❧

Nothing would ever fill the massive hole Kellis's absence caused, but Anna found joy in family visits. Anna and granddaughter Donna Enz Argon were early risers, while LeNore and Marilyn slept late. Donna followed Anna, whom the children called Grandma Hoard, for morning chores.

Every morning, the chickens needed to be fed, the cow milked, and eggs collected. Nearly 90 years later, Donna remembered walking to the barn with Grandma Hoard. Grandmother and granddaughter put on bonnets to avoid too much sun. Anna grabbed the milking stool and perched next to the dairy cow. Out of nowhere, several barn cats appeared, waiting for their breakfast. Donna delighted in Grandma Hoard sending a few squirts of milk to the feline mob.

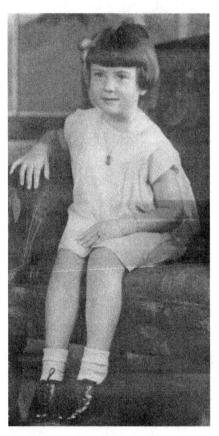

DONNA ENZ AS A CHILD.
FAMILY PHOTO.

Grandma taught Donna how to gingerly reach under a brood hen and check for an egg in the chicken house. Kellis had built a relatively sturdy chicken house, which sat off the ground near the summer kitchen. While most farms are rife with critters, Kellis's chicken house managed to survive animal assaults for eighty years. In the late 20th century, the chicken house met its match when neighborhood teens rode a four-wheeler through the south wall.

"Grandma Hoard always had a huge vegetable garden and had flowers around the house and in the backyard," remembered her granddaughter Donna, "The garden was the best place to be in the early morning, with everything so fresh and not so hot."[117]

Anna and Donna also enjoyed gardening together, and Donna would pursue a lifelong gardening passion. Near the garden was the last of the Maiden-Blush apple trees from the Hoards' orchard. Apart from

---

[117] Telephone conversation, Donna Enz Argon, Bedford, Massachusetts, with author, May 24, 2020.

providing sweet fruit every autumn, the tree had a second job holding one end of the clothesline.

Their tree had come from Anna's Grandpa Reuben Long's orchard up the hill, and the original seeds came via wagon from Ohio, carefully culled by Elizabeth Long in the late 1830s. Reuben's mother brought seeds from Virginia to Ohio in the early 19th century.

"Grandma and I sometimes worked in the truck patch," remembered Donna. "We went out early in the morning to avoid the hot sun. She showed me how to plant, and seed, and gather, how to water, and how to enjoy the first sun-blessed strawberries. I learned the garden was a treasure."[118]

Donna sometimes helped Grandma Hoard with the laundry. When opened, the summer kitchen's front window allowed a gasoline engine's black belt to attach to the washing machine. Grandma had done the laundry with a hand wringer for many years.

"Grandpa Hoard had to start the motor and usually had a difficult time," said Donna. "He needed to swear, but he didn't think he should with his granddaughter there. Even a small child knows these things."[119]

ANNA LONG HOARD, MARILYN ENZ, AND LENORE HOARD ENZ, AT HOMELAND FARM, 1936. FAMILY PHOTO.

Anna's brother, Calvin Long, the last remaining son of Washington and Jane Baker Long, died on June 5, 1934. His funeral service was held at the Eberhard Church, with burial at Eberhard Cemetery.[120] Calvin's daughter Berniece eventually moved to Washington's home at Reuben's original cabin, which sat on her half of the legacy farm.

---

[118] Argon, Donna Enz. Letter to Author. "Dear Amy." Bedford, Massachusetts, April 17, 2010.
[119] Telephone conversation with Donna Enz Argon and author, September 2020.
[120] Calvin Long Succumbs, *South Whitley Tribune*, South Whitley, Indiana, June 8, 1934.

Anna's health stayed steady until late 1936, when she was diagnosed with ovarian cancer. By spring 1937, she had become bedfast. LeNore and the girls spent much time at the farm; by now, Carl's father Charles had invited him into the family business in Fort Wayne. Carl accepted, and the family moved to the farm in 1937, likely when Donna finished school in Springfield.

From her sickbed, Anna could hear the sweet chatter of the small birds in and near the wren house. She could hear her granddaughters' laughter. Anna could smell the purple and white lilac bushes in the yard. Donna and Marilyn often picked flowers for their grandmother, the same bouquets Anna had loved all her life and the same her ancestors had loved. Some were delicate, others hardy, but the flowers survived many generations in nature, coming back every spring.[121]

Anna departed life with her daughters beside her in the home she and Kellis built on the land she loved. At her death on June 30, 1937, she knew she fulfilled her dream of keeping the farm in the family.

Anna died knowing her land would continue to bless her children. However, intangible legacies were the greatest gifts to her descendants— an ethos of hard work, an awe of nature's power and beauty, a heart for philanthropy, and a respect for the common good. Her grandchildren, neither of whom would live on the farm after adulthood, grew as kind and good women.

The family no longer owns the legacy farm or Kellis and Anna's smaller farm. The land was sold in 2010 when the legacy farm had been in the family for 173 years. Caring for others and cultivating the land and community taught many timeless life lessons, lessons still meaningful today, and lessons that will echo for generations.

---

[121] Telephone conversation between Donna Enz Argon and author, April 11, 2021.

Afterword

Legacy land is not a new topic for a book. It was important to me to tell the stories I learned for the descendants of those four families who came to Whitley County, Indiana, before 1840.

When my grandparents bought Anna and Zoe's portions of the farm in the 1930s, my grandmother named her portion of the legacy farm "Homeland," a name that stuck.

Homeland Farm was sold in 2010 after 173 years of continuous family ownership. Today, the only family land in Whitley County is at Eberhard Cemetery, where six generations of the family rest, from Catherine Hiestand Long 1777-1870 to Marilyn Enz McVay 1932-2012.

The stories of the Whitley County pioneers will never die. We remember the generations who worked hard on land they loved. We remember the turn of the seasons, the colorful wildflowers, the stars hung low in an endless sky, and the sound of a wheat crop rustled by a west wind. We remember life was hard in ways we in contemporary life cannot imagine. Somehow, people made it through.

This project has taken me more than two years, though I've been thinking about it all my life. If you asked me when I started, I'm likely to say, "1958," because of notes Grammy left with my name on them and that date. Many remarkable people have contributed their time and encouragement to this project.

I thank my husband and best friend, Randy Abbott, for his continuous encouragement and support of my writing and this project. What writer of narrative nonfiction wouldn't love to have a research librarian as a partner?

A special thank you to my father, William McVay, who loved and cared for the farm and helped me immensely with this book's research. As a child, Dad lived on a farm that still used horses to pull a plow until 1946. He also spent his career in agriculture education, teaching the next generation of agriculturalists. I can't even begin to say how special and joyful this bonus time with my dad has been. He is now 90 years old.

Special thanks to my brother, Andrew William McVay, an expert in things related to the land, especially horses.

Over the years, I noted discussions and kept letters from my aunt, Donna Enz Argon, which have been insightful and helpful. I am grateful for her lifetime of love and support.

Thank you to Mary Kay Fleming for guiding me with her terrific and specific editing skills and Diana Ani Stokely for her outstanding cover design and interior template.

Thanks to Jill Boggs, JaLeen Bultmann-Deardurff, John DiDomizio, Lynda Heines, Joyce Hite, Pam Kiser-Records, Elizabeth Kronemiller, Marty Levine, Wingate Maine, Abby Obenchain, Mark Records, Dr. Christine Riley, Kathy Riordan, Taira Simmons, Barbara Stahura, and Ruth Stanley.

I am grateful for the letters and information received from my late cousin, Priscilla Baumheckel.

And much love to Grammy, shown here holding me at Homeland Farm in 1958.

Bonus: Hot-Shot Women's Basketball

In 1970, LeNore and her lifelong friend Marie Luecke Bridge reunited their 1926 Whitley County Champion Women's Basketball Team. Following are excerpts from the newspaper article after the August 1970 event, held in the Washington Center Community Building (the gym had been removed years before.)

About 25 people, representing girls' and boys' basketball teams from 1926, met for a buffet dinner.

As preparation for the get-together progressed, Mrs. Enz went to the county recorder's office. She secured Xerox copies of newspaper articles in *The Commercial-Mail* in 1926 covering the girls' games played before the tournament. A tape recording was made.

About 25 former schoolmates and teachers heard the newspaper write-ups on tape after the buffet dinner, with Mrs. Enz and Weldon Alexander giving the commentary.

It was recalled that the Washington Center girls had defeated Columbia City 17-16, a week before the tournament, and won the right to meet South Whitley, which the Washington Center girls won 20-16, making them county champs.

Game rules at that time required that a woman coach the girls. If she did not have the experience and necessary training, the coach of the boys' team would assist her with the coaching duties.

The only playing by the reunited team was passing the small gold basketball that decorated the cake down the table to Mrs. Enz, who was delegated to keep all the team's information.[122]

---

[122] Adams, Mrs. John Q. "Dinner Reunites Members of 1926 Girls County Basketball Championship Team: Tape Recording Brings Back Memories." *The Commercial-Mail.* September 19, 1970.

About the Author

Amy McVay Abbott is the great-great-great-granddaughter of Reuben and Elizabeth Long. She grew up in Whitley County, Indiana, the daughter of Marilyn Anne Enz McVay and William Gene McVay, spending much time at her grandparents' legacy farm. Today, Amy is retired and lives in southwestern Indiana with her husband, Randy, also retired. Amy and her brother Andrew are members of First Families of Whitley County.

Amy is the author of seven books and has been featured in three anthologies. She was a newspaper columnist for nearly a decade and has been widely published in multiple local, regional, and national print and online venues. Amy earned bachelor's and master's degrees in journalism from Ball State University in Muncie, Indiana.

Read more about the author at https://www.amyabbottwrites.com.

INDEX

CPSIA information can be obtained
at www.ICGtesting.com
Printed in the USA
LVHW061106190621
690654LV00003B/429